VALUES
AND THE
FUTURE

MODELS OF
COMMUNITY COLLEGE
DEVELOPMENT

JOHN O. HUNTER

FIRST EDITION

ISBN 0-89491-005-1

Library of Congress
Catalog Card Number: 77-72609

BANNER BOOKS INTERNATIONAL
13415 Ventura Boulevard
Sherman Oaks, California 91423

TO TWO WOMEN

MY WIFE, LYLA BETH

MY MOTHER, JANE

Men ought to be educated, not for
the present, but for a possibly
improved condition of man in the
future; that is, in a manner which is
adapted to the *idea of humanity* and
the whole destiny of man.

Kant

The institution which feigns to give
and to require what it cannot is false
and demoralized.

Ortega

PREFACE

Among the nation's community college administrators, the work ethic is in good hands. Pressed by the duties and responsibilities of office, few administrators possess the needed time to articulate in writing the issues and value-decisions that confront them daily. Even after completing this work, Erikson's question hovers in mind: Have I understood myself? I think so.

In these pages, I have sought to present a working administrator's perspectives of community college development, aware that aspects of it are at odds with prevailing concepts in educational administration. The theme "values and the future" was chosen because of the conviction shared by many in higher education that values clarification in community college development has become more important — and problematic — than ever before.

The expansion of higher education as a response to egalitarian forces within society was accomplished in large part in recent decades by the building of two-year colleges. Today, some 1200 such colleges exist in the United States. Most are public *community colleges*. The concept of "community" is central in their philosophy. The continued development of this concept is crucial to any claim of distinctiveness that community colleges may make. Yet it is "community" that is most jeopardized by the trends toward centralization that are most obvious in factors such as accountability legislation and faculty unionism. To redress the balance requires a new philosophical dialogue.

Values, of course, are difficult to define. I am aware of the pitfalls in examining the broad range of topics presented in the following chapters. Since all are invested with value judgments, attaining a holistic perspective is even more difficult. Yet the community college cannot avoid the challenge of such evaluation if it is to continue as a healthy and growing institution in the new era of development which is now beginning. The valuation process goes on both pragmatically and through philosophical inquiry. In both cases, where assertions are made in these pages, they should be read as though ending with question marks, for the stimulation of inquiry and dialogue are cardinal objectives of this work.

CONTENTS

ACKNOWLEDGMENTS

Appreciation is extended to all of the publishers who have granted permission to quote from works cited, particularly the following:

To Oxford University Press, Oxford, for permission to quote from *The Letters of John Keats*, Fourth Edition, edited by Maurice Buxton Forman, © 1952.

To American Management Associations, New York, for permission to quote from William F. Glueck, *Organization Planning and Development,* © 1971.

To G. P. Putnam's Sons, New York, for permission to quote from John Dewey, *Art as Experience,* © 1934 by John Dewey.

To Harper & Row, Publishers, Inc., New York, for permission to quote from Kenneth Boulding, *Conflict and Defense*: *A General Theory* © 1962 by Kenneth Ewert Boulding, and to use figure from Jonas Salk, *The Survival of the Wisest,* ©1973 by Jonas Salk.

To Addison-Wesley Publishing Company, Reading, Mass., for permission to use figure from Edgar H. Schein, *Process Consultation*: *Its Role in Organization Development*, © 1969.

To Random House, Inc., for permission to quote from: George T. Lock Land, *Grow or Die*: *The Unifying Principle of Transformation* © 1973 by George T. Lock Land; Arthur Koestler, *The Roots of Experience*, © 1972 by Arthur Koestler; and *The Philosophy of Kant*: *Immanuel Kant's Moral and Political Writings*, translated and edited by Carl J. Friedrich, © 1949.

To George Braziller, Inc., for permission to quote from Ervin Laszlo, *The Systems View of the World*, © 1972 by Ervin Laszlo.

To Basic Books, Inc., New York, for permission to quote from Marjorie Grene, *Approaches to a Philosophical Biology*, © 1965, 1966, 1967, 1968 by Marjorie Grene.

To University of Chicago Press, Chicago, for permission to quote from Thomas Kuhn, *The Structure of Scientific Revolutions*, Second Edition, © 1962, 1970.

To University of Michigan Press, Ann Arbor, for permission to quote from *Education* by Immanuel Kant, translated by Annette Churton, © 1961.

I owe much to many personal friends and colleagues, whose insights reflect throughout this book. Most of all, I am indebted to my sources: Kant, Dewey, Maslow, Boulding, Becker, Laszlo, and the others whom I have referenced. These are my masters, and I have tried to approach them with humility. At the same time, I have been deliberately assertive on some points, and where I have used theory, it always has been with a theory-action marriage in mind.

While too many people are due recognition to list all their names here, I must mention two whose loyal support and assistance have been invaluable: my wife, Lyla Beth Hunter, and my secretary, Mary Ann Corieri. I also wish to acknowledge the counsel over several years of Dr. Ernest Notar.

I am indebted to the Trustees of Niagara County Community College for a half-year leave, during which time this work was finished, and to the National Association of College and University Business Officers for a leave grant which enabled me to travel extensively, visiting colleges and universities in several states. Every college administrator should have such an opportunity.

John O. Hunter

Sanborn, New York
August, 1976

I

ACCOUNTABILITY AND VALUES

Viewed as a system, the two-year community college may be seen to consist of five major sub-systems: (1) Transformation (curriculum, instruction, counseling); (2) Admissions and Outreach; (3) Budgeting and Finance; (4) Technical Operations and Support; and (5) Evaluation and Development. Linking these sectors is a sixth sub-system, Governance and Management. The primary focus of this work is Evaluation and Development. Obviously, this area cannot be analyzed exclusive of the other interacting components of the college system.

The community college exists within an environment that may be described as four-dimensional: physical (terrain, climate, lay-out); cultural (norms, values, goals of the community and society); political (laws, authority, countervailing pressures); and technological (state of knowledge and instrumentation available to the college for the performance of its purposes.)[1] From this environment, the community college must draw its resources. Since these resources are not permanently fixed, the responsibility for justifying and managing them grows more acute as the internal needs and external support of the college are shaped by various pressures.

Like an organic entity, the community college strives to maintain its integrity in a changing environment, a dynamic impulse. The college contributes benevolently to its environment according to its own relative internal benevolence and dynamism. It is affected, in turn, by the climate of acceptance in the larger system in which it functions. A continuous struggle for adaptation prevails. It is precisely because the community college must maintain a leading edge in the change process that major emphasis on evaluation and development should be integrated into every component of the college system. Particularly as the community college moves from early development to institutional maturity in a "steady state" era, the fostering of evaluation and development programs becomes crucial. Fortunately, adaptive models needed for this purpose are emerging.

1

Accountability

An umbrella term sometimes given to these efforts is "accountability." Accountability in education is not new, but the tide of public dissatisfaction with education at all levels has given it a new urgency. As a general concept, "accountability" is difficult to define because it is used from so many different perspectives and, as a matter of public policy, has little history. In the curricular sense, "accountability" refers to the relevance of programs to student needs and the intersection of programs with the actual work force which students are seeking to join. In the instructional sense, "accountability" means to hold educators responsible for student learning, including skills acquisition, according to the implied promise of such learning in the curriculum objectives. In the community sense, it places responsibility on schools and colleges to respond effectively to the diverse needs of the drawn population, particularly those minority clienteles previously not well served by educational institutions. In the governance sense, it requires the adoption of regulations to guarantee equality of opportunity and "affirmative action." In the business sense, it assumes efficient management of resources, eliminating waste and extravagance, and ensuring the cost-effectiveness of the educational enterprise. Finally, in the professional development sense, "accountability" raises questions about the obligations of professional staff beyond teaching for the continuing growth and development of the institution which they serve. In every sense, the main focus of accountability is on outcomes. This raises a number of associated measurement problems.

Educational problems are inter-institutional, involving the family, community, and mass media as well as the schools and colleges. For example, the declining level of literacy among entering college freshmen is noted. The public schools are admonished to do better, and post-secondary institutions are challenged to pick up the illiteracy problem. The schools, however, are caught, in turn, by forces beyond their control — sharply rising divorce rates, single-parent families, child neglect — all pointing to the decreasing influence of the family in preparing children for learning and fostering educational values. At the college level, commitment to the problem is closely tied to the availability of resources and time. Remedial instruction is expensive, requiring a counseling dimension as well as a curricular approach. The schools are failing, and at the post-secondary level, at least, the community colleges are obligated by their missions to assume the remediation role. Yet the inter-relatedness of the institutional sources of the problem

creates obstacles which are indeterminate in educational accountability.

Making educational institutions more accountable, therefore, is a
complex mandate. It is fitting that schools and colleges should be called
upon to assume the leadership for a reformation. Community colleges
may be justly expected to play a major role. Unfortunately, however,
the call for accountability, particularly as it resonates from a corporate
ethic, does not assess the main strength of American education, which
is found in the diversity of its institutions.

At the post-secondary level, accountability is both a positive and
negative force. In its best form, accountability is a drive for reasoned
change *within* organization and administration. In its worst form, accountability pushes for uniformity and centralization which conflict
with the natural patterns of humanistic educational reform. In this
counter-productive form, which is dominant, the constructive processes of change are seriously undermined by the draining away of faculty
and administrative time and energy in legal and technical functions,
which, though necessary to carry out, do not provide direct educational service.

Legislated Accountability

The emergence of public accountability, so replete in higher education
legislation of the 1970s, is due not only to concern over the cost-
effectiveness of programs or response to new clienteles, but, more
broadly, to the lack of clearly articulated directions of development
wherein institutions of higher education have failed to demonstrate
vision and leadership in constructing the future of the community and
its work force and of society at large.

It is not adequate to say that higher education contributes to new
knowledge. Indeed, at the community college level, few can make that
claim. As a teaching institution, the community college finds its identity in community education and community service. Thus, to remain
vital, the college must not only monitor change, but must contribute to
enlightened prognosis. A community college draws a small circle.
Therefore it is more vulnerable to the immediate forces of its environment, and, unless it keeps a perspective on the future of the community
and a corresponding management of the college resources, the college
becomes ever more subject to provincial claims and attitudes.

While it is obvious that the community college must be accountable
in this general sense of providing effective instruction and of contribut-

3

ing to the community's welfare, serious questions arise about the meaning and process of accountability when it is specifically legislated. Such legislation can be more troublesome than ameliorative when applied to the college governance. For example, a major new clientele for the community colleges in the mid-seventies were Vietnam War veterans. Support legislation and Veterans Administration directives mandating "standards of progress" and follow-up studies on employability seem on the surface merely insistence on responsible education. What is not calculated at first glance, however, is the cost to the college in meeting the bureaucratic regulations. Even more serious is the intrusion on autonomy in academic affairs. The impact of such regulations on the college administration can be significant since it is forced to reconcile external demands with its own indigenous strategies for conducting educational programs and institutional research.

This comparatively mild example reflects a basic orientation to accountability in education which, though well intentioned, represents a danger not only to the autonomy of community colleges but to the cause of educational reform. The problem in this kind of accountability is not the escalation of the administrative paper chase, which probably can be eased in time through bureaucratic compromise or better synchronization of management information compiles. The real problem is with the analytic predication which gives impetus to accountability.

What right has the community college administrator, trained to observe the primacy of public needs and demands, to argue against accountability? Does not the community deserve for its increasing tax dollars the best management possible? Of course it does. The problem begins as a matter of definition. Accountability to whom and for what? What is the larger purpose and the general result?

Values Crisis and Bureaucracy

The preceding questions call for an inquiry into the comparative or contrasting values of education and bureaucracy in American life, a task which is too ambitious to undertake here. The state of the community college as it copes with accountability does require, however, some comment on the values crisis occurring in American society. This crisis is reflected in its educational institutions, where it works against the standardization implicit in the desire for greater bureaucratic control and efficiency.

The challenge of traditional norms and roles in sex, religion and authority is diffusing so rapidly that it cannot be defined or under-

4

stood as a counter-culture force. Rather, it is a change in the entire social fabric, so that the values crisis is also an institutional crisis. An aspect of this dual crisis is reflected at the college level in the growing concern about future work opportunities. Young adults, especially, are seeking meaningful jobs which allow synthesis of life-style and work commitment. The inability of the professions, public service and the corporate sector to satisfy these needs, combined with the uncertainty of schools and colleges in preparing students for the work world, has brought us to a critical turning point in our social history.

The "job crisis" may be seen as more than a symptom of institutional failure. Beyond the job markets are deeper spiritual problems stemming from a way of life achieved by an enormous rape of nature in the name of industrial progress. It is a way of life founded on the notion of abundant and cheap energy. The materialistic values system which has resulted cannot be sustained without continued exploitation of energy' resources. Even with this exploitation, its products, such as the automobile, have not contributed to greater individual choice or enhanced community life within our disintegrating cities. Urban sprawl and blight are the results. The conglomerate tendency has required bureaucratic evolution, but bureaucracy does not represent a steady hand at the helm.

Accountability policies implemented by bureaucratic means are aimed obliquely, at best, at the process of social change and educational reform. As Bennis has pointed out, the evolution of bureaucratic theory and practice has not resulted in "typical bureaucrats," but neither has it accommodated changes in society, particularly in those trends regarding interpersonal relationships and human potential development.[2] Recognizing the bent of bureaucracy is not akin to engaging in the sociological pastime of denouncing bureaucrats. There is probably no such phenomenon as the "bureaucratic personality," but there is an organizational style (not unique to federal and state bureaus) which is geared to impersonal, categorical decision-making.

Since bureaucracy is essential in a technology-intensive society, it must have continuity. But, without assuming that the community college can withdraw from formal organization, what concerns the college is the capacity to envision and to implement a concept of community life in which interpersonal relationshps and group concensus are optimized. Granted, there may be tension between an emphasis on meeting individual needs and the demands of the organization, especially in regard to resources. Community does not mean absence of conflict. There is, nevertheless, a philosophical commitment in the very origins of the community college to those values of personal growth and community experience which are not always measurable or discernible through empirical analysis.

Several studies of formal organization reveal the objective basis of the bureaucratic management style. Rational administrative models to implement economy and efficiency codes set the framework for planning that does not admit humanistic styles and judgments which are empirically unverifiable. Efficiency is posited as the highest value. The rationale is not blind to questions of morality but depends almost wholly on the expressed values of society, not as changing but as historically determined. The exclusive reliance on rational models is inadequate to cope with current change. Programs and policies produced are therefore likely to have counter-intuitive effects.

Bureaucratic ineptitude has caused widespread concern, but public policy has not yet shaken this cold embrace nor accepted a new consensus. Much of the action in the name of public accountability is predicated on the prevailing bureaucratic perspective which now confronts education head-on.

It is fair to argue that higher education would not be in such a defensive position today had its self-regulatory systems been more effective in the past. The necessity of advancing the effectiveness of programs is not disputed. Adaptation to new economic constraints and the need for managerial efficiency are not the issue. They are merely an aspect of institutional evaluation and development. Nor is this mini-critique a plea for an anachronistic concept of local autonomy. Colleges, like individuals, are not free always to do as they please. The governing structure of a larger education system, in which most community colleges operate, may require regional conservation and linking practices which are normal in systems development. There is a difference, however, between planned inter-institutional cooperation and imposed external authority through legislation.

A survey of higher education was undertaken by the American Council on Education in 1968 on the probability and desirability of 35 hypothetical events or developments in the next decade. Ranked among the top 10 in probability was an increase in statewide coordination. The same survey, however, indicated a low probability of collective bargaining becoming a widely adopted method of determining faculty salaries and conditions of employment.[3] Near the end of the decade which was the subject of the prediction model, there is an increase in state and regional coordination efforts. But in spite of these efforts, which hold greater promise of protecting autonomy and diversity, there is a more vigorous increase in management legislation and collective bargaining, both of which lead to centralization and greater external authority. The inability of ACE members to foresee these developments illustrates perhaps more than anything else the system shocks which are now being felt.

Higher education collective bargaining is just about a decade old. Its impact is being felt more pervasively at the community college level than elsewhere. Accountability legislation, on the other hand, is affecting university governance more seriously. Yet both of these developments are realities for the future of high education at all levels. Both create a billiard effect as educational leadership is bounced away from strictly educational concerns, such as academic programs and missions development. While community colleges have not yet experienced the legislative effects of accountability to the same degree as the universities, the trend is clear. The community college may claim a different line-up of political supporters and antagonists, but it is all the same game. The community college does not have much history, and, as it has been less tested institutionally, in some ways it is even more vulnerable to the new forces.

Politicians are fond of saying that those who pay shall call the tune. Political power has always been a reality in the community college environment, enjoining the enfranchised constituency with the professional base of the college development in a more or less dynamic mode and attesting to the spirit of democratic involvement. When the politically intuited needs are translated through centralized, external authority, however, mediation is lost. Legislated accountability threatens democratic involvement as it threatens educational diversity.

Some observers may see in the trend to centralization an escape from the local harassment that sometimes seems unbearable as it rends legitimate collegial purposes. They may see the gains of an efficiency ultimately attained. It is questionable that increased external authority can achieve efficiency in an educational institution, but even with this outcome, Thoreau reminds us that "You never gain something but that you lose something." What the community college stands to lose is a significant role in the invention of its own future. There must be a better way through new patterns of governance that seek reasonable accommodation and fitness without surrender of autonomy and which reconstitute broad-based educational leadership within the organization.

Modeling

The surge of accountability through legislation and bureaucratic standards has stimulated modeling of evaluation and development or change systems. In a pragmatic sense, modeling is merely the attempt to visualize all of the increments in a path of change. Lippitt explains: "Unless a planned change effort is organized in terms so simple and clearly related to each other that the mind can grasp them, it will frequently remain incomprehensible to those involved in the change process."[4] This is keen advice for community college administration and faculty as they seek to generate a conceptual framework for evaluation and development.

Community colleges have common goals, but the differences in locale and community subculture are often significant. The history and "institutional ethos" of the college are additional factors in determining the nature of the change process within the organization. Models, therefore, are not easily transportable from one college to another, though there are benefits to be derived from experience-sharing. Just as a road map is not the system of roads it describes, so a model does not necessarily encapsulate the realities of what is happening or even the totality of what should happen. As a guide, it is a means of gaining a holistic perspective. But, as the beauty of a lake is not described in a map, so it is with the relative quality of organizational efforts.

There are many different types of models. The road map is a graphic model. Examples of physical models are the planetarium, building replicas, and the chemist's model of an element. Prescriptive models forecast developments or the consequences of events that might occur. Descriptive models explain events or phenomena. Simulation models mathematically project an equation of input variables and measure the effect of changing a variable in the equation. Cybernetic models trace inputs, outputs and resulting feedback in a closed loop form. Heuristic models are analyses that seek to discover similar qualities or relationships between objects. The types and functions of models and modeling may be described endlessly without serving administrative purposes. Modeling is not an end in itself.

The task of modeling evaluation and development in the community college organization requires that three areas be brought into view: (1)

the allocation and utilization of financial and physical resources, (2) programs and policies, and (3) human resources. Without dismissing the first two areas, the emphasis throughout this work is on organization and human resource development and the attainment of a gestalt-values perspective in any modeling attempts. In this latter mode, evaluation and development concerns the individual, the group, and the organization as a whole. Applications are sought from the field of Organization Development.[5] The pattern may be seen as one of expanding circles placed within an environment which influences the process at each focal point:

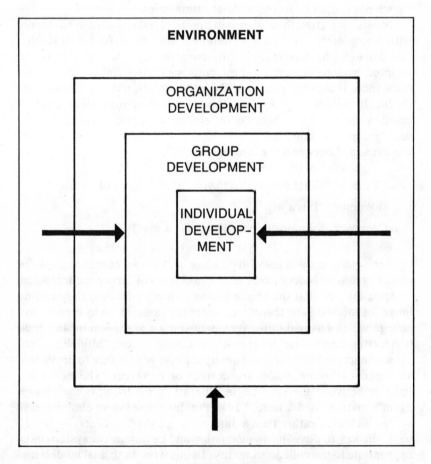

Figure 1.1

It is easy to fall into the error of focusing too strongly on sophisticated models which, though comprehensible, may not be attractive to professional staff who are not systems oriented. Much confusion surrounds modeling efforts in curriculum and teaching/learning evaluation as faculty members are asked to become familiar with terms such as "mission," "behavioral objective," "criterion reference," and "measure of performance." As one Department Chairperson forthrightly expressed it, when evaluative work is rendered too complex and time-consuming due to this verbiage, the process is likely to collapse under its own weight. In-service seminars aimed at introducing educational science may be a valuable contribution to the staff development program, but the science cannot be forced without stultification.

Models may grow through group practice, but to become enamored with completely worked up, detailed models is to fall into that rationalistic trap associated with bureaucracy. Administration so tempted becomes aware of the faculty's nearly infinite capacity for resistance. It also happens that the administration may be ready and the faculty willing, but somehow the positive intentions become obfuscated by the revolving shades of difference in the realities perceived by each group. The communications situation that results is like that of the exchange between the two women:

1st Woman: "What did you do to your hair? It looks like a wig."

2nd Woman: "It is a wig."

1st Woman: "Strange, it doesn't look like a wig."

These qualifications notwithstanding, there is an essential place for model building. Indeed, one of the problems of larger technological systems may be that they have become so complicated, they can no longer be modeled and therefore cannot be managed. (Any community college which has had difficulty establishing a Management Information System appreciates this point.) As Lippitt states, "Modeling is not yet a science and neither you nor anyone else will be able to prove that all aspects of your model are correct or incorrect. The necessary balance between the science and the art of modeling is the change agent's mature confidence."[6] Taken in this sense, as an evolving task — "an endeavor rather than a thing accomplished" (Keats) — modeling is the key to devising an evaluation and development system most appropriate to the college's identity. In this work both goal models and system models are useful in providing a context.

Summary

The community college is viewed as an organic system embedded in a larger system. Constant change is assumed. As the competition for resources to promote higher education becomes stronger, constraints and demands on the college from external agencies and groups are growing. Accountability has become public policy, resulting in management legislation, the intent of which is to foster greater efficiency and educational responsibility. Bureaucracy influences the development and execution of this legislation. Questions are raised about values in education (for example, diversity) and their compatibility with values in bureaucracy. Educational centralization and external authority are seen as negative forces which have the effect of generating ever greater technical and legal workloads on college administration at the cost of academic disorientation. Accountability, however, like collective bargaining, is a reality in the community college environment which must be faced. New patterns of governance must be developed which seek a reasonable accommmodation while conserving autonomy as much as possible. In the search for new patterns, models are emerging. Some cautions in modeling are urged. A model adopted by one college is not necessarily appropriate for another. The question of faculty receptivity also must be considered. Modeling is, nevertheless, the key to building evaluation and development systems. Attention is turned to goals and systems.

GOALS AND SYSTEMS

Models for organization and administration are developed from various persuasions and viewpoints. Of the contending approaches, Management by Objectives seems to be the most rapidly ascending. MBO has been established as a trend in many business organizations, probably due, in large measure, to the seminal work of Peter Drucker who first outlined the concept more than 20 years ago.[7] The Deegan and Fritz workbook, *MBO Goes to College*, provides a detailed description of the MBO model for applicability to higher education administration.[8]

Many community colleges are employing modified versions of MBO. Under President Robert Lahti, William Rainey Harper College has established leadership in its adoption as a complete administrative strategy. Lahti has based much of his innovation on principles stated by Odiorne, who provides the following definition:

> Management by objectives provides for the maintenance and orderly growth of the organization by means of statements of what is expected for everyone involved, and measurement of what is actually achieved . . . It stresses the ability and achievements of leaders rather than their personality . . . In brief, the system can be described as a process whereby the superior and subordinate managers of an organization jointly identify its common goals, define each individual's major area of responsibility in terms of the results expected, and use these measures as guides for operating the unit and assessing the contribution of each of its members.[9]

Deegan and Fritz give the following operational definition for colleges:

> Management by Objectives is a continual process whereby superior and subordinate managers of the college periodically identify their common goals, define each individual's major areas of responsibility in terms of results expected of

each and use these agreed-upon measures as guides for each operating department and for assessing contributions of each manager to the work of the entire institution.[10]

Lahti comments:

The system reinforces the principle of obtaining the best efforts from both the individual workers and from the managers of working groups. MBO permits greater control of managers over their operations and encourages improved subordinate-superior relationships as a result of joint participation in goal-setting and planning.[11]

The claims of increased productivity, innovation and morale attributed to MBO by its advocates are impressive.[12] There is much to recommend the MBO approach,and much to be learned from it for application in any administrative structure. For all its hazards, some of which are surmised here, MBO may be the only salvation of college administration facing collective bargaining in the future.

It should be noted that there is considerable difference between making a commitment to MBO and borrowing from it as a way of thinking. In the most accurate sense of implementing the MBO model, it must be undertaken fully by the organization, for it is a complete management system. Its advocates are clear in warning that MBO implementation requires considerable competence and energy. As a model, it is not suggested to be fail-safe. Not from the temerity of offering a critique so much as to raise the question of values in community college administration, the attempt here is to compare MBO with an alternative developmental approach which is given greater priority.

Preliminary Conceptions

There are, of course, many issues in evaluation and development, but as a platform for examining a community college's potential and readiness to adjust as well as its performance, the following are first suggested as salient questions:

1) What is the college doing, and how well is it performing its stated missions?

2) How can the college's developing needs be defined, organized, and "squared up" more sufficiently with the total human resource potential it has for meeting those needs?

3) What developmental activities are necessary for obtaining a fuller awareness and realization of the human resource growth potential?

4 What programmatic changes and resources reallocation are necessary to cope with changing community needs and workforce realities?

5) How can the college become more flexible and streamlined in its internal control procedures?

6) How can the college publicly communicate its performance and accountability with integrity so as to maintain community support and confidence in a time of constricting financial resources?

A corollary for each question is: "Are we moving ahead in acting on this basic question?" Underlying each of these questions are people concerns. It may seem trite, but in a holistic sense, evaluation and development in the community college seek to answer a simple question: *what is happening to people in the college*?

The foregoing questions, then, focus more on process than on goals. Granting the importance of goals-setting to institutional development, the primacy belongs to the values in the struggle to achieve these goals and to reassess position constantly. Implicit in these questions are matters of personal commitment and abilities, resiliency, radical insights, responsibility, and integrity—enduring values. There is bias here for an open and flexible framework for organization development that permits new things to be seen in different ways and, though futuristically oriented, tries to allow for the unexpected. It is an option for a fairly lean set of prescribed arrangements that is sometimes uncomfortable, probably because it lacks a high degree of regularity. For want of a better term, it might be labeled a "natural systems" approach (Gouldner).

There are two defenses for the "natural systems" alternative to the more rigorous structural activity of Management by Objectives. The first lies in recognition of the uncertainty of planning in higher education institutions confronted by environmental instability. While this argument can be inverted to demonstrate the efficacy of MBO, it is presented anyway to raise the point that college administrators are not prophets and seers. In this respect at least, they are not unlike corporate executives:

> We set goals and draw up budgets. We establish a control
> system that let's us know when we're off plan so we can
> correct the deviation. Just when we think we're in fine shape,
> we run into some problem from left field that knocks us way
> off course.[13]

Impacting events cannot be pinpointed, but it is likely that events
significantly impacting governance shall occur, and it is possible to
develop early-warning signals if the administration meets certain
requisites.

If there were no focus on adaptability and contingency planning, the
"natural systems" approach would represent only the usual "crisis
management" — when, all of a sudden, the totally unexpected hits and
"We're in the soup again." It is more than that, however. Viewing the
organization as subject to internal "reaction processes" (Boulding)
and external forces not completely foreseeable, there is a deliberate
attempt for goal production *short of optimization*. Without this room to
maneuver, a college administration which is understaffed (as is usually
the case in community colleges) is likely to suffer constant tension and
a resulting drag that affects morale of the entire organization, no matter
how well its objectives and activities may have been planned. For this
same reason, in the implementation of the strict MBO model, objectives may be deliberately set low though the process goes on; but this
lack of "stretch" is a fault in the management system which aims at
maximizing the effective use of resources. Otherwise, the time consumption of the process is not justified. How does the administration
guard against too much short-fall? Obviously, judgment is required in
administration as well as supervision.

The second defense lies in the view of organizations as being naturally conflict-oriented. MBO gets at this problem, too, but in a different
way. Conflict in a business corporation, which has different "products" and rewards potential, is not the same thing as conflict in a
collegial institution.[14] Participants in college governance, especially
faculty, tend to image the organization as a collection of individuals.
The image may be disputed, but it has some bearing on the management of objectives. Conflict can be creative, particularly when
it concerns ideas and, therefore, may symptomize a healthy state of
the organization if it is not so dysfunctional as to cause acute disorder.

The challenge of administration is to mediate the conflict so as to
move toward harmony. As Boulding says, "The essence of the drama
of conflict is likewise its resolution. It is not the conflict as such that

15

makes the drama but the resolution of the conflict as a meaningful process through time."[15] This conflict resolution might concern objectives, but it could just as easily concern non-goal, valuing activities. For example, two departments might agree on the objective of introducing a new program and on the sharing of resources required to achieve it but disagree strongly on competing methodologies. It becomes an argument over quality, a philosophical consideration.

Decision-making concludes these disputes, but it does not necessarily resolve them. (Old administrators, tell us that, years ago, while these battles raged on, the decisions could be made quietly, and the faculty never knew the difference.) Every decision leads to reaction as well as to result. The hope is that the reaction will be mature, as may be expected from professionals who understand that a decision had to be made. If the organization is healthy, the decision will be respected as a rational outcome even as it is perceived to be wrong. If the decision is indeed "wrong," of course, other qualitative effects may be felt.

It may be that the organization simply has relied upon its constitutional processes, another sign of health. Nevertheless, such decisions cannot be planned in advance. Yet, as they occur, they naturally shape the organization. There are many assumptions here, of course: decisiveness, fact-finding, proper timing, and respect for the decision-maker(s). The major point, however, is that, as administration works in this problem-solving milieu, the difficulty is not so much in determining objectives, supervising, or making decisions as in the *thinking through* to the possible consequences of the decisions and objectives in motion. Where the organization is small, as in community colleges, the distance between the actors and reactors is not great. Integrity may suffice in most cases, but, at times, even the best laid plans go astray. Of course, the argument here is not that these intricacies of behavior should preclude clarification of purpose. Keats still is preferable to Burns:

> I go among the fields and catch a glimpse of a field-mouse
> hurrying along. To what? The creature has a purpose, and
> his eyes are bright with it. I go amongst the buildings of a
> city, and I see a man hurrying along. To what? The creature
> has a purpose and his eyes are bright with it.[16]

MBO and Natural systems

The comparison between the MBO and "natural systems" approaches may be seen as a distinction between goal models and system models.

16

Etzioni points out that, in a goal–model approach, success is defined as "a complete or at least a substantial realization of the organizational goal."[17] The system model, on the other hand, "explicitly recognizes that the organization solves certain problems other than those directly involved in the achievement of the goal, and that excessive concern with the latter may result in insufficient attention to other necessary organizational activities, and to a lack of coordination between the inflated goal activities and the de-emphasized non-goal activities."[18]

The social system of a college exists as a result of the history of group interactions and ongoing activities. All systems have goals which are tempered by a constant mix of values — values in flux. The selection of a system model over a goal model as a means of interpreting the system or introducing change factors does not mean necessarily that a more accurate measurement of values is obtained nor that a keener sense of direction is provided. From the research point of view, the system model is more complex. Likewise, however, the selection of a goal model does not indemnify the organization simply because goals and goal-strategies are clearly focused. In both models, an emphasis is on communications, but communication about what?

The goals of any social system either are derived from or induce values. Organizational values are not always consociate with the values of groups or individuals affected by goal activity. How difficult it is to separate goals from values! Values are not beyond the scope of a goal model such as a fully established Management by Objectives, but the approach is different from that of natural systems. In MBO, emphasis is placed on the precise identification of parts of the system, job descriptions, the production of well formulated, clear and specific objectives, and monitoring devices. The structural activities focus on goals, not values.

Part of the style of the natural systems approach is to be a respecter of many different "styles" and interests. Synergy is the word-ideal. Theoretically, at least, evaluation does not take individual style into account unless it is clearly dysfunctional, in which case, even then, personal growth is sought rather than conformity. The evaluation methods seek to enhance the dignity of individuals as well as institutional integrity. The stylistic thrust is to emphasize professional growth that brings its own creative results and rewards and often springs from unforeseen opportunities grasped. Serendipity is hoped for. The resulting administrative structure, while providing authority and chain of command for normal decision-making, attempts to decentralize

17

authority and suffuse responsibility as much as possible, not as a means of "democratizing" the organization but of making it flexible. *Ad hocracy* and voluntarism are relied upon in programs and policy development. The effectiveness of the approach, therefore, depends vitally on professional maturity and responsible decision-making at every level. The freedom value is on freedom *to* do something rather than on freedom *from* elaborated expectations and requirements. To the extent that these ideals compare with a "participative management" emphasis in MBO, the two approaches may be compatible, though not in practical effects. (A theoretical commonality is discussed in Chapter Four.) The crucial question, of course, is how does the organization create social opportunities for collaboration and growth?

It is interesting to note that MBO technique usually requires that statements of objectives begin with the preposition "To." The natural systems approach, in contrast, stresses "between" rather than "to," recognizing that implementation of "To do X" may result in doing X', or in some problem-solving cases, even "to do Y."[19] MBO presumes that systems are modeled rationally and that failure to carry out an objective according to its prescription is a failure in the rational system. There is not much reliance on intuition nor predilection for coming at activities from different angles without forecasting results. One should not be surprised.

It may be argued that the MBO approach is more stabilizing, neater, better organized, and much more efficient. While it may be all of these things, the model may not sufficiently grasp the complexities of organization development in higher education. The difference between the perspectives on development can be illustrated graphically. MBO, essentially, is knowing exactly what must be done and proceeding to do it. Thus, it is like a straight line or linear path:

In contrast, a natural system model not only recognizes but embraces the tangential starts and stops. Thus, it is like a more cluttered critical path:[20]

Figure 2.1

Important to both approaches is the work of master planning. Regular updating of specific institutional goals is the fulcrum of MBO operations. Likewise, the absence of a master plan and directional reports would deplete a natural systems approach so badly that monitoring would be very difficult. "Natural systems" at its best is not just "muddling through," a characteristic of those administrations which do not strive for a conceptual framework. Again, however, there are degrees of difference in the values ascribed to master planning. "Natural systems" presumes organic development. An organic master plan provides a basic sense of direction and seeks to evoke responses. It is a catalyst for growth and stops there. An MBO master plan becomes a record on which to score pluses and minuses. Is the future invented, or is it planned?

Of course, it is necessary to continually articulate needs, objectives, and intentions. If one knows what he or she is doing, one should be able to communicate it. One also should be able to mediate any problems that result from overlap or strain on the resources available for continuing what he or she is doing. What is true for the individual is even more true for groups and for the organization as a whole. Obviously, then, much depends upon the planning approach.

Optimal Planning

Plans come from planning and planning is a process. Planning is emphasized in MBO to the extent that it goes on at every level of work within the organization. Institutional goals are explicitly stated which represent the organization's claims to allegiance from all its members. Working within the pattern of institutional goals, each unit leader is responsible for setting the objectives of his unit. To enhance a sense of obligation through "ownership," the process of establishing the objectives should include the unit members' participation. The precision, however, is a leadership function. The precise statements form part of the justification for going on with the larger missions of the organization.

Each unit's objectives must be defined in terms of the larger unit of which it is a part. The objectives are subject to review and approval of higher administration, and the resources necessary to carry out the objectives must be considered at both levels. The MBO adminisrator may employ the technique of suggesting additional objectives, a shortened time frame, or altered priorities as a means of pressing for optimal performance.

The unit leader is responsible for accomplishment of the objectives. Therefore, he or she is obligated to follow-through activities. Evaluation centers on whether or not these objectives are met. Since the accomplishment is based on a standard of performance each objective must be stated in measurable terms. Therefore, some uniformity in producing the objective statements is required. MBO training is necessary for writing good objectives. Thus, while an appraisal of the need "to develop community education programs" may provide rationale, it must be accompanied by measurable statements to make the leap from rhetoric to management objective.

> Example: To develop the community education program, by doubling the enrollment in the credit-free sector, with an overall faculty-student ratio of 20:1, in the coming academic year.

The accomplishment of the objectives also may require "force field analysis" (Lewin), that is, the identification and analysis of internal forces which may promote or hinder the planned change effort. It is in this vast gray area that the MBO approach must go well beyond planning if it is to be successful. At first glance, MBO appears to be a deceptively simple concept. Yet, as Deegan and Fritz remind college users, MBO is a "total system of management, an attempt to incorporate all the things a manager ought to be doing into an organized effort."[21] To not adopt the full scale model may be a formula for failure. It is this very claim of totality, however, that warrants a closer inspection. Are the nuggets in MBO worth investment in the whole mine?

In MBO, as in other models, management is both an art and a science. Its art is realized in a leadership eye for obstacles to be overcome and in human relations techniques which are motivational. Its science is in the objectivity of the planning process and the measurement of results. While the total achievement of objectives is not expected, the planning takes a path of optimization.[22] Administrative aggressiveness overlays the entire schema. According to Odiorne, MBO is characterized as the "success ethic" itself. In its application to the business world, at least, MBO brings success, and rewards follow. Odiorne contends: "In the best-run corporations, more people are clear as to their objectives than in less well-run, less successful organizations."[23]

The pre-eminence given to planning in the MBO model sets the style of the administration which adopts this approach. Planning and organization development are not mutually exclusive, but some of the differences in emphasis are worth considering. Melcher and Glueck have given attention to these differences. Melcher provides the following definitions:

> There are two different approaches: *organization planning*, which focuses on the analysis aspect, and *organization development*, the guidance aspect, which often involves resolving sensitive interpersonal and intergroup relationship problems.
>
> Organization planning is involved with reviewing and evaluating, on a continuous basis, all organization entities to determine whether the missions, structures, functions, and responsibility relationships are clearly defined and understood and effectively coordinated to facilitate the overall objectives of the company.
>
> Organization development is providing counsel and guidance that aid and encourage management to develop and clarify its organizational missions; to delineate and effectively group the work to be performed; and to clarify and resolve responsibility relationships that will enable both the organization and its people to realize their mutual objectives.[24]

As Glueck further explains, organization planning places emphasis on structure to divide the work, relying on administrative coordination to bring order to the whole. For the most part, people are expected to adapt to the structure. Organization development, on the other hand, places emphasis on people first and seeks to formalize effective working relationships by building on the informal structure. For this purpose, T Group training and other developmental activities are introduced which receive more attention than the "structural activities" associated with planning.[25]

Since planning always presumes resource allocation to staff development, and, conversely, organization development presumes at least a modicum of good planning, obviously the emphasis on planning as differentiated from development is a matter of comparison rather than of contrast.

Adaptive Planning

One's vision of the future influences one's perception of the major developing needs of the organization. Forecasting is always risky business which makes long-range or strategic planning much more of an art than is short-term planning. Therefore, it is mainly conjectural to conclude that organization development is more crucial than planning to the future of the community college. This perspective does not obviate planning, but it does introduce a concept of "adaptive planning" (Tonneson) rather than "optimal" planning.

The first lesson to be learned from MBO by the community college educator is the need for understanding as clearly as possible the missions of the college. (The term "mission" has various definitions. For the working definition used here, see Figure 2.2 and the example that follows). Missions are derived from the enabling legislation of the community college, but only in very broad terms. The college catalog usually contains a statement of institutional philosophy which references basic purposes, a statement which probably deserves more continuing care than it is usually given. The first task in adaptive planning is to invent, from the general statements, the more specific missions which may be ascribed to integral groups within the college and which, through a bonding process, mold the identity of the college. Mission statements give life to abstract purpose statements.

For example, the college may assume a fine arts mission:

> The fine arts mission is three-dimensional, since its goals are: (1) to offer specific programs for students who seek formal education and training in one or more of the art fields for the purpose of pursuing the arts as a profession or as an avocational interest; (2) to contribute to the means for aesthetic experience by all members of the college community and to enhance their understanding of the essential place of art in society; (3) to contribute to the cultural enrichment of the community at large by providing public programs (concerts, exhibits, and so forth) of excellent quality on a regular basis.

If fine arts is truly a college mission, it is not a separate enclave of activity but becomes a characteristic of the college's transformational system. As a college-wide investment, it is fostered through relationships between the Fine Arts program and other programs, such as Student Government and Continuing Education. The successful implementation of the mission depends on the leadership of a "psychlogical group" (Schein), which is formed as a result of formal organization and relationships that emerge informally. The mission relates to a drive for deeper and wider consciousness.

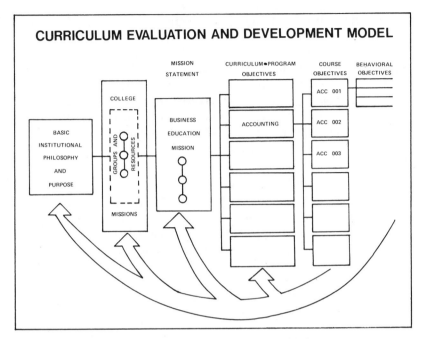

Figure 2.2 Curriculum Evaluation And Development Model

Terms

1. **Mission**—reserved for the inherent purposes of a group or sub-system within the college representing an integral philosophical component of the college (without reference to administrative structure).
2. **Curriculum**—an academic system of credit-bearing courses, required or elective, the satisfactory completion of which leads to a degree or certificate.
3. **Program**—an entity of courses and/or activities which are naturally related and are identifiable as such.
4. **Goals**—reserved for broad purposes as applied to the institution as a whole, such as in Master Planning.
5. **Objectives**—reserved for purposes of a particular curriculum or program.

College Mission Examples

Allied Health
Business Education
Fine Arts
Health and Physical Education
Social Sciences
Technologies
Admissions
Counseling
Learning Resources
Remediation

Fine arts is usually a high-cost program. In a time of declining resources, a fine arts mission which is seen to be a department or discipline function only probably will not last long; nor should it, for, in this case, the discipline has been cut off and isolated from the larger educational goals of the college. In its lack of imagination about the organic place of art, the discipline has contributed to the puritan notion of art as a "frill." So it is with most disciplines that adopt a static outlook on the learning system in which they are involved. At the same time, the mission development may be subjective as well as objective. To teach art aggressively may not be unlike to teach aggression artfully.

What gives the Fine Arts department greater meaning is its leadership participation in the Fine Arts mission. In the formal structure, the department (or other named unit) is, of course, a key element. The department has a sapiential authority which is necessary to define the mission. The mission definition is a continuing task of adaptation as well as of knowledge application.

From missions, curricula and programs are derived, which, in turn, generate courses. A systemic/analytic framework for defining, relating, and evaluating curriculum and course objectives is necessary for the development of existing curricula and the planning of new curricula. The model is relatively simple.[26] (See **Figure 2.2**) Too often, in the community college, courses are proliferated with no clear justification when weighed on a scale of specific curriculum objectives. It is easy to build courses. The challenge lies in building strong relationships between courses, the curriculum, and the controlling mission. The systemic analysis should stimulate modularization and adaption of co-curricular activities.

Much emphasis has been given in recent years to the development of behavioral or performance objectives so that student achievement may be more effectively measured. This activity also can be incorporated, but it is secondary to the development of a conceptual framework by which the behavioral concentration may be clearly adapted to the holistic endeavor. Behavioral objectives are more easily achieved in some courses than in others (for example, in accounting as compared with history).[27] The stress in adaptive planning is on a free creative environment in which greater definition is constantly encouraged. But, as the whole remains "greater than the sum of its parts," there is a tendency to shy away from mechanistic techniques.

Organic Master Plan

The emphasis on missions development need not lead to goals dis-placement. It is necessary to assess institutional needs and to set goals in order to continue with a sense of direction in the college's activities. Goals-setting becomes increasingly important as the college matures.

During the early development of a community college, professional commitment and enthusiasm may be nurtured through shared appraisal of that development. The growth is obviously noteworthy. With in-crease in physical size and complexity of governance, however, the sharing becomes more difficult to sustain. Growth is more difficult to measure. It is easy to see, for example, that a doubling of staff size does not merely double the potential number of communication exchange routes and, therefore, of perceptions and interpretations. The pos-sibilities are raised geometrically:

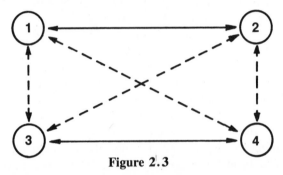

Figure 2.3

In this new situation, it is questionable how extensive the participa-tion in planning can be by all groups affected by the planning results. Participation in governance and goals-setting moves into a representa-tive mode. A central committee may provide representation in planning if it is carefully created and charged. Ideally, it should be representative of the three principal groups of the college — faculty, administration, and students — and probably should include *ex-officio* membership, at least, of higher administration.

Needless to say, any such arrangement is fraught with hazards. The question of how to lend administrative guidance to a faculty-induced change effort without becoming dominant is a constant concern in the OD administrator's mind. (This problem exists, however, only in a shared authority model.) As one of the most important vehicles in the formal structure, the committee must receive strong support and en-couragement from higher administration in order to function effectively. At the same time, its integrity must be respected. If the committee is perceived to be a tool for administrative manipulation rather than for inducing change, its efforts will fail. Where such circumstances cannot be mitigated, it is wiser for the administration to back off and move to other matters.[28] The faculty must bring an equal share of maturity to the process.

The goals which are periodically established usually are presented in a master plan which is meant to have a duration of four or five years. Obviously, to write a master plan which is submitted to higher authority and forgotten is an almost meaningless and expensive exercise. (There is always some value in the philosophical dialogue that transpires with planning committees, though this dialogue also may prove to be enervating if not brought to conclusion.) The plan is meant to become a working document. It also should be recognized that planning is a continuous learning process: each new plan is an improvement on the previous in quality and format.

In adaptive planning, the master plan goals are largely subject to interpretation and priority selection: (1) Rationale is provided; (2) units responsible for making the plan work continue to set priorities and to provide strategies; and (3) the implementation provides feedback for continuing the process through unit directional reports. A master interim progress and revision report also may be prepared and distributed. It is a closed loop model. (See **Figure 2.4**)

The planning should achieve a balance of traditional aims with more radical forecasts and needs assessment. In this sense, it is future-oriented but based on past achievement and identity. Analysis of institutional and environmental trends provides the context in which goals are set. The resources picture is very much a part of this analysis. Effective planning, of course, requires information about the college and its environment. Institutional research must be well tuned into the process.

If a committee is used, it must know its materials and understand the work commitment required. It is a permanent committee, responsible for monitoring results as well as for determining goals. To prevent a routinization of the effort and consequent loss of vitality, the membership should change periodically, perhaps in a staggered fashion.

The central committee may seek guidance from external resource groups and agencies (for example, regional planning boards) and internal subcommittees to assess needs or to analyze special problems. Those groups responsible for implementation also must understand the process in order to give full seriousness to their task of responding to the directions of development provided by the planning documents. Thus again, communication from the administration and faculty leadership is a chief factor in the process.

The resulting master plan most likely will contain a variety of goals, some of which are extrinsic to the faculty's main interests or responsibilities. For example, a goal related to the need for improvement of a technical operation, such as student registration, may be applauded by the faculty though it is an administrative charge that does not involve them directly. The response to the cited need is left largely to an administrative department. Interfacing usually is required on these goals. This category might be labeled *support goals*.

A second category includes those goals of transformational system development which may be given uneven treatment, according to group priorities, without inhibiting movement toward such goals. These are *programmatic goals*. For example, a goal to establish field experience or internship programs may need to be pushed more strongly in one area than another. Its cogency may apply throughout the system, but success does not depend on uniform achievement. It becomes a question of mission development.

The third and most critical category is that of *innovative* or *structural change goals* in which the response cannot be fractionated. To achieve the goal requires a total mobilization. For example, to reconstruct all courses for a schedule of modular offerings and a new academic calendar, college-wide cooperation is required. These goals cannot come to fruition without a carefully built consensus during the drive to which loud protest is virtually certain to occur. The administration and the master plan committee must be prepared accordingly.

In this third category, prioritization is essential. The master plan should address these priorities clearly. The number of such goals also must be carefully weighed. Too much ambition in this area can have catastrophic effects on the health of the organization. If a condition of entropy is thought to exist, it may be the intent to break and remold the system through the introduction of several structural change goals. Such an attempt would be alien to the organic plan concept, however, and, therefore, not likely to occur in adaptive planning. To arrive at consensus on these goals, a greater number may be entertained than finally would be permitted. Therefore, these goals should be filtered through the college governance system to allow the opportunity for debate.

The final plan should be approved in its totality by the college trustees as well as by the professional base of governance, presumably a representative senate or council or a faculty union. During this final stage, leadership skills are the cutting edge of results. Faculty leaders are needed as much as the administration, but it is the administration that must communicate the plan externally and resolve any divergencies between the groups involved.

Some features of this approach are not necessarily disjunctive with those of an MBO model. The requirments of the latter would lend more specificity to the means of obtaining the objectives and to the measurement of results. For this reason, MBO would be transcendent.

It will be seen that the explication here of missions development and goals-setting draws mainly on academic affairs, supposedly the faculty's most natural area of strength. Let us assume, however, that the faculty cannot do it alone — indeed, cannot even get started. Then, clearly, there is a role for academic administration in this work; and, just as clearly, if administration is constantly being diverted to other assignments, this work simply will not get done. (If MBO could reestablish academic priority, it would be immensely more attractive.) Organization development places heavy responsibility on middle administration (deans, division/department chairpersons) to provide both catalysis and mediation.

It is just as clear that the administration cannot do it alone. The old cliché about faculty and life-blood is no less valid even if it sometimes gets only a dull echo. What conditions are necessary for teamwork? How does the organization create social opportunities for collaboration and growth? Subsequent chapters continue to explore the amelioration of this problem. In this exploration, attention first must be given to the issues and models of formal evaluation.

Summary

Organization models are presented as being either goals-oriented or systems-oriented. MBO is discussed in the former context, and "natural systems" is discussed as an alternative. The comparison is aimed at raising values. Administrative leadership is vital in either approach, though the administrative styles differ. MBO is seen as a total management system from which there is much to be learned and which may be a necessary trend in higher education. Preference is given to the "natural systems' approach, however, which is suggested

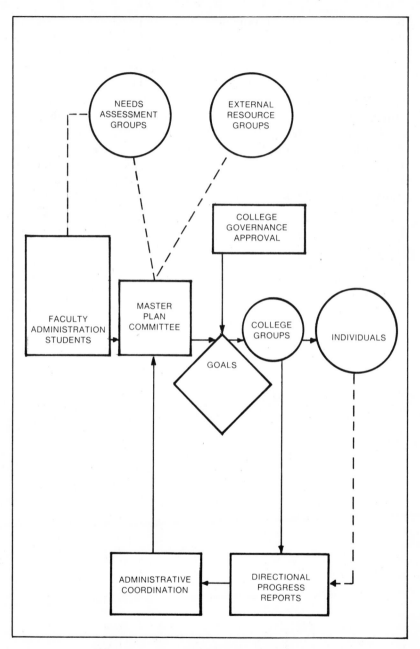

Figure 2.4 Master Planning Model

to be more in keeping with the need for an emphasis on organization development as differentiated from organization planning. MBO is discussed as a framework for "optimal planning." Again focusing on the values of adaptability and flexibility, "adaptive planning" is offered for comparative purposes. The latter is exemplified through missions development, which is seen as a holistic endeavor. A conventional systemic/analytic model is presented to show more clearly the relevance of courses to curriculum/program objectives and hence the relationship to the college's identifiable philosophical missions and basic purposes. The master plan as a centerpiece in developmental activity is discussed in detail. A master planning model also is presented. Attention is turned to formal evaluation.

III

FORMAL EVALUATION

The story is told of Oppenheimer, who, when asked for an opinion about the effects of reformed science education on graduate students, replied that he had no views on the subject because, "you see, I am only concerned with about 10 of them." Community college faculty cannot afford the luxury of being concerned with only 10 students, but, appropriately broadened, their major responsibility generates a viewpoint not entirely unlike Oppenheimer's answer. It is well known in the field that community college faculty generally do not contribute to research. As teaching faculty, their professional concern is almost entirely with students, which also may explain why major issues impacting the welfare of the college are not always followed nor understood. Only the most outstanding, versatile faculty members are as well versed in governance issues as they are in their teaching obligations. While community college faculty are "generalists" rather than "specialists," there are limits to the knowledge of institutional development they may be expected to have while devoting attention to individual student welfare and the teaching-learning process.

Communication of an overview of institutional development is both possible and highly desirable for maintaining integrity, but the chief professional interest of the faculty is with what helps directly in the classroom. Toward this end, evaluation becomes a pragmatic consideration. Does it help me? Does it help students? Evaluation of this sort goes on all the time, for the most part informally. The crux of the difference between evaluation and accountability lies with these pragmatics.

Formal evaluation of outcomes, resources management, and staff performance requires a systematic approach. It requires quantification and reliance on technology — those elements of administration that some faculty cannot recognize as having much to do with student life. The disdain of these elements, however, reflects a weak perspective on the complexity of relationships between individuals and groups in any

31

modern organization. For establishing institutional claims and a sense of direction, formal evaluation is essential, but successful implementation requires clear models.

The models suggested here are less sophisticated than is called for by the current state of the art. In regard to measurement, they are intentionally incomplete: while a few specific instruments are named, an attempt is made to omit mention of choice of instruments. All evaluators understand that formal testing requires a determination of validity, reliability, and discrimination of the instrumentation according to the population to be tested, though, in the end, the selection of what to do and how to do it more often results from intuition than is generally acknowledged. In recent years, skepticism has arisen about the ethics of testing and the accuracy of personality test-assessments especially. Freedom of information laws are another factor of general concern. A college must weigh those considerations in deciding what testing programs should be introduced. Structure of the models also is open to challenge, for, as in collective bargaining, what one college needs or can afford may not be needed by or affordable to other colleges even within the same region.

Management Information System

On the technical side of the evaluation process, the college needs well ordered, digestible information about the utilization of its resources and its outcomes. On the social side, it needs to know how to use the information in the change process as it is compiled. It is relatively easy to adopt formal instruments and devices which produce volumes of information, but information is not knowledge. Knowledge of what is happening requires analysis of the information and communication. The problem usually is not with lack of information but with its organization. The model, therefore, must address not only the types of information needed but the appropriateness of involvement by individuals and groups in its analysis. In other words, formal evaluation is more a social problem than a technical one.

All colleges have a "Management Information System", whether formally developed or not. However, there can be enormous inefficiency in the system if it has not been modeled. The basic questions are:

(1) What kinds of information do we need?
(2) Who needs it and in what form?
(3) How do we get it?

All of this discussion is practical. It relates to the practical ends of administration rather than to information theory. Therefore, the use of the term "information" refers only to data acquisition and data flow. There are assumptions that, at the end of the process something happens — that the information will lead to improved decision-making, or that policy will be better related to programs implementation as a result of information (feedback).

Obviously, computing services are the heart of a well-developed MIS. Essential functions such as cost analysis cannot be done without the computer. Some of these functions could be handled through regional computing services, however. It is not necessary for the college to invest heavily in large-core computers in order to carry out these functions. A system of mini-computers may serve the community college's needs better if lines are established to outside vendors for the more complex forms of information retrieval.

There are six categories of information required in the MIS:

1. Statistical: Information obtained from standard records on employees and from the student data base, relating to male/female populations, age groups, enrollment figures, academic averages, and so forth.

2. Student Research: Information on persistence and attrition, changing nature of student population, student needs (for example, level of reading and writing skills), and graduate follow-ups by program (transfer success/job placement).

3. Financial and Budgeting: Information on program costs, support service costs, plant operating and maintenance costs, FTE ratios by program, faculty loads, salaries, and benefits.

4. College Environment: Attitudinal information from all internal groups about college responses to their needs, perceptions as to college goals, and organizational health.

5. Community and Work Force Research: Information on job markets and changing business/industrial requirements, economic conditions, shifting populations (for example, in-migration compared to out-migration), and community group needs.

6. Facilities Usage: Rooms occupancy figures, percentages of usage in specified time periods, and usage by outside groups.

The information needs expressed in these categories are not all equal. Priorities must be established and production schedules set. Since the information is sought for management or developmental purposes, priorities are established by asking why it is needed. If no valid answer is given, the item should be dropped. Facilities usage, for example, may be very important in program planning for one college and not at all a concern in another. If the answer is solely that an outside agency wants the information, it may be valid enough but not reasonable, and, in a healthy organization, the request would be challenged. Out of this conflict should come either a better understanding of the larger MIS in which the college is participating or some relief from its pressures. Accountability reporting is a fact of existence, but accountability does not loom larger than the total college life.

The first three information categories are increasingly important for accountability. The responsibility to external authority undoubtedly shapes the college's MIS as adjustments are made to accommodate particular deadlines and report formats. If it is the only shaper, however, distortions creep into the information which go uncorrected because of the mechanical nature of filing information. For example, external reports often call for attrition figures. No single percentage of attrition has much meaning. Attrition is a complex phenomenon which includes vagaries not easily detected and legitimate questions as to when attrition is really persistence according to another growth experience sought and, therefore, an element for the positive side of the ledger. By typical educational accounting, attrition is looked upon as a decidedly negative feature, but, while attrition always ought to be a concern, attrition analysis is one of the most difficult drawers to open in institutional research.

A better approach to the use of attrition information, perhaps, is to fit it into a tracking scheme which accounts for program changes and inter-institutional transfer. The MIS should be well enough developed to provide a print-out of all students in a program at any time and, upon further inquiry, references to any previous program experience by students in the college. This feature provides up-to-date information on enrollments as well as on program losses and gains. If a student profile is made for each student upon entering the college, other attrition factors may be identified for specific programs, such as reading test scores, high school prerequisites, firmness of commitment, or social needs. If the counseling staff is large enough, exit interviews should be arranged for all students dropping out, with appropriate information entered in the student file. Some students, of course, are only "step-outs" and may return. (A longitudinal analysis of this process could be useful for developing hypotheses about maturity and student values in relationship to program changes.) This information is not likely to be complete because students usually do not follow neat program patterns. (For example, a student listed as a matriculant in one program may have elected most of his or her courses in an entirely different program). Nevertheless, it can be useful as a dimension of programs evaluation and perhaps for an assessment of student values.

Any research performed on student values or needs should involve pre- and post-testing in order to obtain information on outcomes. Some of this information can be obtained semester by semester in easy fashion (for example, by surveying remedial reading test scores.) Surveys, however, require careful preparation, sample selection, and timing. The college environment and community surveys may be spread over a longer period, perhaps two years, without losing synchronization. One of the major problems with surveys, of course, is getting a good return. Fortunately, surveys are only one aspect of evaluation, and sometimes, the least important aspect. The effort, therefore, should be planned for a smaller part of the total time investment to be used in collecting the data and the larger part in data analysis. The analysis moves the effort into a communication mode which takes on dynamics not found in the mere collection of data.

Follow-up studies for all programs should be annual in order to analyze the consistency of program results and trends. If they are begun in early Fall, results may be reported by January so that they may be used as part of an annual updating of programs. Follow-up studies are crucial, of course, for gaining significant knowledge of outcomes. Outcomes analysis is a bridge between academic planning and financial planning.

If all of this seems exceedingly dull, it is due to the technical nature of information-gathering. Yet, clearly, a community college which cannot acquire the information it needs for evaluation and development is operating in the dark. Efficient Data Processing is a key to efficient college management. Management specialists and technicians therefore have an increasingly important role in the college operation. There are times when other members of the administration must wait upon the services they provide, knowing that these services are the springboard to an integrated approach to college development.

But MIS is not evaluation and development! It may be necessary to make MIS the top administrative priority until the technical operations are smoothed out,[29] but to place the college at the mercy of those operations is to go in the wrong direction. Avoidance of this is part of the social problem of MIS development. EDP-user conflict is at the heart of this problem, the resolution of which should not to be left to group consensus nor to arbitrary decisions by management specialists (such as the Director of Computing Services). Because making a successful (though not smooth) transition to an MIS is important, this area of major conflict requires constant mediation by higher administration, at least until a single plane of communication is achieved.

The EDP users, of course, are those staff members whose requests for information have been prioritized according to the model of college evaluation needs (ahead of, rather than after, the computer model). Except for program follow-up studies, which ought to be a main concern of academic departments, student research may be placed primarily in the hands of the counseling staff. Community research may be assumed by a continuing education office. There are, of course, various possibilities, depending upon the size and character of the organization.

If an analysis is conducted consistently, the results should be useful in a growth sense to the group which is doing the analysis. Beyond group benefits, the analysis may need to be communicated to other groups if it is to have a significant impact. Ultimately, it should be fed into the institutional planning process. There is the same danger, however, in trying to communicate analytic results as in gathering too much information. It may fall on deaf ears if attention has not been paid to social relationships. An administrative coordinator (for example, the Director of Institutional Research) who is familiar with the entire system should have the responsibility of pooling the results as they unfold and assisting in the communication — a considerable challenge, but one shared by higher administration.

Cost Analysis and Productivity

In the current surge of accountability, much is being said about productivity in public sector organizations, including colleges. Despite the prevailing lack of expertise on the subject, seminars and workshops are being conducted to train administrators in how to measure productivity. Particularly revealing are U.S. Department of Labor publications on the topic, in which the criteria and standards are notably quantitative. The message is clear enough, but the whole area of investigation is tangled and confused. Unfortunately, there isn't much help even in defining the problem of how to measure *productivity* in an educational institution. The word itself has a strange ring; the basic definitions are difficult to apply.[30]

There is a developing science of simulation, however, which may contribute to a partial understanding. Among its products, the National Center for Higher Education Management Systems includes the Resource Requirements Prediction Model.[31] The core of the model is the Induced Course Load Matrix. This matrix presumes organization of faculty by discipline and fields of study which are mutually exclusive but which, appropriately adapted for the community college, can provide program costing information. NCHEMS is well known in the field, of course. A number of community colleges are now experimenting with the RRPM model. NCHEMS staff members warn that the utility and impact of the model takes time and that a college ought not to adopt it without careful preparation. Indeed, it should not be considered until the MIS is well developed.

A similar model is CAMPUS, developed by the Systems Research Group at the University of Toronto.[32] These and other simulation models look promising for administration if they are allowed to take hold naturally and do not become confused in the question of productivity. Cost-simulation models provide information for cost-analysis. It is important in academic programs evaluation to distinguish between cost-simulation and cost-analysis on one side and *cost-effectiveness* (or cost-benefits analysis) on the other. *Cost-simulation* is the use of information for charting the actual utilization of resources and measuring the effects on the whole of changing an input variable (for example, the effects of decreasing enrollment in a particular program). Cost-simulation does provide some information on productivity, but it does not provide a bank for the balancing of outcomes. In other words, while cost-simulation models may be very useful in cost-analysis, they do not clear the hurdle of values to cost-effectiveness.

In the simplest terms, *productivity* is defined as "output over input," — that is, the yield from the resources and energy used. By this definition, it may be possible to obtain some indication of *cost-efficiency* in an educational institution through quantitative measuring devices if there are comparative standards of efficiency (for example, the number of graduates in different programs equally resourced). However, *there is no way to measure cost-effectiveness in an educational institution.*

Cost-effectiveness is primarily a qualitative matter in which value-judgment is controlling. If effectiveness were very narrowly defined (for example, the number of graduates who are placed in the employment field for which they are trained), a measurement would be possible, though, even then, the effectiveness may be perceived differently by the employer. The important point, however, is that education is not merely training. For the same reason, it cannot be precisely ascertained whether increased expenditures will raise the quality of programs, though there is evidence to suggest that the relationship between expenditures and quality is positive. It also is no longer clear that the benefits of education may be measured in terms of increased earning power.

The state of the art may develop, but the challenge is appalling. Gross has suggested that non-quantifiable phenomena, such as human satisfactions, may be measured quantitatively by using "surrogates", that is, "indirect-indicators that serve as quantitative substitutes for, or representatives of, the phenomena we want to measure."[33] Perhaps this has some potential, but the present spinning about the need to measure everything as a means of evaluating productivity is not merely self-defeating; in educational institutions, at least, it tends to obscure rather than to sharpen purpose. How does one measure excellence and a commitment to excellence?

An over emphasis on measurement can lead to short-term results at the expense of long-term needs, for productivity assessment does not yield information about needs. Needs assessment is an area in which quantitative information is joined with qualitative judgment.[34] A plurality of needs may be identified through the MIS. These needs must be weighed against each other in the process of which other quantitative information (for example, program costs) is used. The bottom line, however, is subjective judgment as to what will fly and what will not. Cost-effectiveness students, of course, seek to remove the subjectivity, or at least to reduce it sharply. (It would be interesting to know how many chief financial officers in community colleges agree that it can be done.) In these matters, the administrator must keep a foot in both the quantitative and qualitative camps. The academic administrator, at least, keeps his or her best foot in the qualitative. The objective here is to move steadily toward a deeper consideration of the quality problem.

Since qualitative concerns cannot be subsumed by quantitative measures, it becomes necessary to shift from cost-effectiveness to another concept — that of organizational effectiveness. This shift is not merely a play on words. *Organizational effectiveness* refers to the process of identifying the missions and goals of the college (see Chapter Two, Adaptive Planning) and their accomplishment. From this perspective, the MIS is subsumed. Greater attention is given to values dialogue as an end in itself, rather than as a means of productivity, and to organization development techniques. (This theme is explored further in Chapter Four.) The purpose here is to address these concerns in an evaluation model. The model synthesizes professional staff evaluation and programs evaluation.

Programs Evaluation

Given not only the demands of accountability but the tightening of budget constraints, formal evaluation of programs moves into the center of the   OD arena, calling for management emphasis at least equal to the emphasis given to staff evaluation. The model suggested here holds to the assumption that curriculum development is a primary responsibility of faculty but, given the changing needs of students and the continuing changes in all fields, that there is a strong need for outside consultation and assistance in the evaluation process. Outside groups which have suddenly discovered the community college and are eager to supply it with their services often are more hindrance than help. Yet, competent consultation sought for specific purposes can provide an additional stimulus for professional growth as well as a useful evaluation of program quality and future needs.

The key element in the model is an adequate and clear set of procedures for periodic review of specific programs. [35] The model also may incorporate institutional research and cost analysis data, thus providing another mode of data analysis. However, since the model is aimed primarily at qualitative judgment and faculty interactions, its implementation does not depend on MIS development.

An external panel of curriculum consultants is chosen for a two-day evaluation visit. Prior to the visit, the faculty unit assigned to the program prepares a brief self-study report which reviews objectives, resources, and outcomes, much in the same manner as a self-study for accreditation. A file of documents relating to the curriculum is prepared or updated. During the visit, the panel consults with the faculty, students in the program, and administrators related to the program. Classrooms and laboratories are visited. The panel seeks a perspective on the program's *strengths* and *weaknesses* and strives to provide *suggested new directions*. Immediately following the visit, a written report is submitted by the panel with findings presented under these headings. Some of the questions it addresses are:

1. Is the need for the curriculum justified? Is it clearly related to the college missions?

2. Are the curriculum objectives valid? Are proposed curriculum directions appropriate, considering the needs of students and the fields for which they are being trained?

3. Is the curriculum content current? Do the courses relate well? Is there an integrated basic skills component?

4. What are the students' perceptions of the overall quality of instruction? Of their needs satisfaction? Is there evidence of good rapport with faculty?

5. What are the professional aims of the faculty? Is there evidence of academic vitality?

6. Does the program enjoy sufficient support from the administration and other support areas (for example, the library)?

7. Are sufficient resources available to support the program? Are existing resources and facilities appropriately and well used?

8. Are there any obstacles to the continuation of the program?

Following receipt of the consultants' report, the faculty unit should have an opportunity to respond. Group meetings may be useful for continuing the dialogue so that maximum benefits are received from the consulting experience. The quality of the consultation, of course, is a factor in the success of the experience. A good consultant is an effective change agent. Therefore, the panel must be carefully chosen.

Perhaps the best approach is to assume that there are no experts in curriculum consulting, but that there are respected colleagues in other institutions and experienced field professionals. A formal policy statement is necessary to provide for team selection, visit preparation, reporting, and so forth. The faculty unit may be expected to suggest individuals whom they believe are qualified to evaluate the program. If two or three outside professionals are selected from this list and one faculty member from within the college is appointed, a balanced team should be formed of workable size. There are likely to be residual benefits from including a college representative from another program on the team.

The model also may serve as a stimulus for regional development. If the main consultants are appointed from outside the region, an observer might be invited from a sister community college in the area. The observer should be working in a similar program. If consultant fees are fixed at a reasonable level, several programs might be evaluated each year at a modest cost. The number of programs to be evaluated annually, of course, is related to institutional size.

The initiation of such a model may activate some feelings of insecurity. For the most part, however, community college faculty tend to reflect confidence in their instruction. If it is made clear that the purpose is to provide consultation rather than merely a critique, this confidence should be reinforced. The faculty's self-interests are served: the formal evaluation of programs has become a necessity for communicating not only the strengths of the college but its honest commitment to curriculum problem-solving and change.

Program Commitment and Priorities

The question of continuing commitment to the college's well-established programs arises more frequently as new needs and decreasing resources are analyzed. The possibility of retrenchment obviously has become a nagging factor in the development of many colleges. Without a base of strong, positive development for determining priorities, retrenchment is a serious threat to the college welfare and could lead to disintegration. Effective evaluation of programs and staff development can assist in the reallocation of resources, but letting go of some programs seems implicit in this reallocation. How are priorities determined?

This task, more than any other, requires a synergic relationship between faculty and administration. Chapter Four examines the concept of synergy in greater detail. Suggested here are some criteria for assessing the impact of programs. (See **Figure 3.1**). The use of the matrix requires qualitative judgment as well as quantitative information. It effects a means of using evaluation results in determining priorities, but any such scale obviously assumes a mature posture on organization development. There is no magical solution to the task of prioritizing commitments, for these commitments are laden with human values. But, with no means whatever for beginning this work, the college faces the danger of losing control to external authority, which may weigh the values far less carefully. The criteria suggested relate primarily to internal assessment. Additionally there may be regional considerations, in which the role of external authority is not only legitimate but probably necessary for more effective institutional articulation. The emphasis here is on the maintenance of the college's integrity as it participates within the greater system.

Faculty Evaluation

In the past five years especially, new emphasis has been placed on faculty evaluation and development. A great deal of literature is available on the subject.[36] A number of teaching evaluation instruments have been developed which are more fully "systems" than the older variety of forms — that is, they enable a matching of cognitive styles and teaching methods, or a comparison of the instructor's self-perceptions with the perceptions of others.[37'] Student ratings are the main concern, but some of these new systems include peer and administrative supervisor ratings as well. These are encouraging developments, of course, which have stimulated a greater awareness of formal evaluation benefits. The advisability of conducting some form of student evaluation of courses no longer seems to be seriously in question. In addition to providing information for the improvement of instruction, student ratings effect a necessary privilege. Well used, they also increase student involvement in academic affairs.

The issue of the effectiveness of student ratings in improving instruction is not closed, however. Fortunately, the research continues.[38] As formalized rating systems are used more widely, particularly if public education policy should mandate faculty evaluation, a new environment for this research will be created. What happens when the use of a ratings system becomes routine? When a college opts for mandatory ratings in all courses, there may be a Hawthorne effect at first, but, in time the counter-intuitive effects of the policy are seen as routinization sets in. Some vitality may be preserved by varying the instruments and the schedule of their administration, but the maintenance of vitality depends primarily on faculty desire to use the information. As a first step toward systematic evaluation, student ratings are very helpful, but it seems inadvisable to insist on their continual use. In some cases, an instructor may benefit much more from a personal video-tape of teaching. There are, of course, other opportunities as well, such as exchanging class visits, which need not be elaborated.

A second caution is that student feedback reflects mainly the effectiveness of teaching styles and methods. Even those studies with objective criteria of teacher effectiveness (that is, what students have

FORMAL EVALUATION

PROGRAM IMPACT CRITERIA

1. ACADEMIC MISSION IMPACT

Least Vital to Mission	Well Related to Mission	Well Related & Vital to Mission	Most Crucial to Mission
Duplicative and may be subsumed	Non-duplicative but not well integrated	Unique and well integrated	Unique, most dynamic and well integrated

2. CURRICULAR IMPACT

Least Supportive of Other Programs	Supportive of Other Programs	Essential to Other Programs	Most Supportive and Essential
Highly dependent on other programs	Dependent on other programs	Independent but related to other programs	Most independent

3. EVALUATION IMPACT

Informally Evaluated Inconclusive Results	Formally and Informally Evaluated	Consistently Evaluated with Significant Change Results	Most Exemplary Evaluation Effort
Least proven or recognized	Well recognized program activity	Strong reputation	Most well recognized & highly proven

4. ENROLLMENT IMPACT

Low Clientele Interest	Declining Enrollments	Consistently High Interest and Stable Enrollments	Increasing Enrollment Prospects
High attrition	Normal attrition	Good persistence record	Highest persistence record

5. WORK FORCE IMPACT

Poor Employment Outlook	Marginal Employment Needs	Promising Future Needs	Excellent Employment Outlook
Poor placement record	Satisfactory placement record	Consistently strong placement record	Best placement record

6. INTER—INSTITUTIONAL TRANSFER IMPACT

No Transfer Function	Some Difficulty with Transfer	Good Transfer Articulation	Excellent Transfer Record and Prospects
Unsatisfactory or no transfer follow-up	Satisfactory transfer record	Well recognized success in transfer	Most highly regarded transfer program

7. COMMUNITY IMPACT

Unresponsive to Community Needs	Responsive to Particular Needs of Community	Significant Impact on Community	Most Responsive and Greatest Contribution
Program faculty inactive and unknown in community	Faculty active in outreach	Faculty well known by particular groups	Faculty highly active on behalf of program and college

8. RESOURCES IMPACT

Inadequate Capital Resources	Adequately Resourced but Future Capital Expenditure Required	Well Resourced for Present & Future	Excellent Equipment and Facilities for Present and Future
Inadequately staffed	Overstaffed for current needs	Adequately staffed with enrollment expansion possible	Adequately staffed for current and future needs

9. OPERATING COSTS IMPACT

Lowest Overall Costs	Lowest FTE Costs	Highest FTE Costs	Highest Overall Costs
High costs, low FTE	Low costs, low FTE	High costs, high FTE	Low costs, high FTE

10. GENERAL FUTURE IMPACT

Long Service Program Facing Obsolescence and Stagnancy	Well Established but Inflexible and Past Oriented	Well Established, Flexible and Creative	Well Established, Bright Future Prospects
Recent addition, lacks direction and commitment	Recent addition, developing satisfactorily	Recent addition, strong development and commitment of future	Recent addition, bright future prospects

Figure 3.1

actually learned) do not approach the problem of the relevancy and currency of the performance objectives. (Granted, in a skills course such as typing, this is not a serious problem.) Since students are not on the leading edge of knowledge, they cannot be expected to judge these qualities in the subject matter. Peer evaluation, not necessarily formal, does get at this problem, of course, provided there is a climate which highly values academic interactions. Combining with an equal concern for student rapport, a critical approach to the course/curriculum conent is the major responsibility of all departments, outweighing all other responsibilities and interests. (Chapter Six explores why subject matter is a more important concern than teaching methodology, though, of course, the two are related.) If this caveat is accepted, dialogue moves into consideration of those professional activities — workshops, consultation, and the like — which relate to academic development.

Group Primacy

Whatever the research may conclude about the correlations between the use of rating systems and instructional improvement, the results must vary with the individual. The individual instructor needs sustenance greater than his own proclivities, particularly as the years go on. This sustenance is found through group membership. *The group is the basic unit of change within an organization.* It is through a group process that missions are developed and through interactions within the group that the desire for individual growth is best reinforced.

A college may reflect an institutional ethos, but it is not likely to have a unified learning climate. Learning climates are created by the departments identified with the different curricula according to the primary department's vitality and cohesiveness, but also according to its relationship with other departments. Thus, Secretarial Science may be strong, but its curriculum alliance with English may be poor. Ultimately, any weak department or weak connections between departments involved in the same mission, such that a psychological group has not been formed, have a deleterious effect on mission accomplishment.

Group evaluation is possible through the application of Organization Development techniques. T-Group training is well known, but there are other instruments as well for lifting a group out of itself, so to speak, for a look at how well it functions. For example, in discussing criteria of group maturity, Schein suggests a questionnaire which members may use periodically as a means of engaging in group self-analysis.

CRITERIA OF GROUP MATURITY

1. Adequate mechanisms for getting feedback:
Poor feedback   1 2 3 4 5   Excellent Feedback
mechanisms   Average   mechanisms

2. Adequate decision-making procedure:
Poor decision-   1 2 3 4 5   Very adequate
making procedure   Average   decision-making

3. Optimal cohesion:
Low cohesion   1 2 3 4 5   Optimal cohesion
         Average

4. Flexible organization and procedures
Very inflexible   1 2 3 4 5   Very flexible
         Average

5. Maximum use of member resources:
Poor use of   1 2 3 4 5   Excellent use
resources   Average   of resources

6. Clear communications:
Poor   1 2 3 4 5   Excellent
communication   Average   communication

7. Clear goals accepted by members:
Unclear goals -   1 2 3 4 5   Very clear
not accepted   Average   goals - accepted

8. Feelings of interdependence with authority persons:
No   1 2 3 4 5   High
interdependence   Average   interdependence

9. Shared participation in leadership functions:
No shared   1 2 3 4 5   High shared
participation   Average   participation

10. Acceptance of minority views and persons:
No   1 2 3 4 5   High
acceptance   Average   acceptance

Figure 3.2
Source: Edgar H. Schein, Process Consultation: Its Role in
Organization Development
(Reading, Mass.: Addison-Wesley Publishing Company, 1969.)

(See **Figure 3.2**). Group and individual relations occur in a setting which is both rational and emotional. The task of group evaluation is to create openness and "authenticity" (Argyris) which allows both rational and emotional communication on ideas, problems, and issues. Reasoned change is sought, but interpersonal relationships are never entirely rational. Honest group evaluation looks at the combination of rationality and emotionality, thereby offering a diagnostic tool for change and for maintenance of integrity.

Stagnancy does not set in suddenly in a department. It gradually takes hold because of the ascendancy of provincial attitudes and barriers to self-renewal. These barriers are best removed by the group itself. Isolated individual evaluation is not a wasted effort, but more important is the attention to group dynamics, out of which individual evaluation and growth are continuously stimulated. Administrative leaders play a catalytic role in these affairs and, indeed, may become directly involved in conflict-resolution. But it is a mistake to assume that intervention from the top down is an effective evaluation technique for motivating professional growth.

It is difficult to underestimate the controlling influence on the organization of group development. As the remedial role of the community college emerges more clearly in the face of a continuing decline in literacy scores nationwide, what means does the college have for making the necessary commitment to remediation? It is unrealistic to assume that major additional resources will be made available, yet the future of the community college seems embedded with this problem. The values of general education lie with the basic skills of reading and writing; even math remediation seems related to reading. The problem may be seen as a great opportunity to revitalize general education; indeed, the community college may be the last defense against increasing erosion of the values and skills imparted by general education. Yet, crucial to the whole process is the mobilization of groups for the undertaking of these missions through evaluation and development.

Because the remediation problem is so great, individual faculty efforts fall short of amelioration, and individual evaluation does not always reveal the sources of failure. For example, is the chemistry instructor evaluated on how well he teaches chemistry or basic math? Nor can a vitalistic approach be found in separate, added-on remedial courses placed with a single faculty group. This approach presumes that diagnostic testing is a reliable means of separating students who are ready for college from those who are not. But suppose half or more of the student population falls below a readiness indicator (assuming that such a composite score has meaning even though regional norms differ)? Such a situation is developing for many community colleges, and, in these straits, the college cannot use the elitist concepts which underly the term "remedial." The term "remedial" works against the grain of general education and belongs in the refuse heap of outmoded concepts. To put it another way, all general education, if it is genuine, has a remedial function requiring the commitment of all groups involved in missions development.

Basic skills development is but one example of the primacy of groups within the total college system. As a system, the college relies on liaison between groups, a network function which its administrative staff constantly monitors. Evaluation obviously applies to this group as well.

Administrative Staff Evaluation

Concerning academic administrators, at least, administrative staff evaluation is not a substantially different problem from faculty evaluation except that it is becoming more difficult to specify a congruent range of duties for each administrative office. The job description may not correspond with the exigencies of daily administration. More frequent definition of roles and functions is perhaps the first step in evaluation.

Power and authority are concepts which must be considered in the evaluation of administrative officers. These concepts, of course, are surrounded by many issues. From an OD perspective, the administrator is evaluated not just on his achievement of goals, but on how he achieved the goals and, therefore, on how he used authority to the benefit of the organization. As Levinson illustrates, it is possible for an administrator to achieve goals through personal endeavor and exercise of his or her authority while weakening the organization at the same time.[34] If the values of organization development are accepted, it is unacceptable for the administrator to declare, "All I am interested in are results."

If both the means and the ends are important, then the task of evaluation is, of course, more complex. A four-dimensional approach seems advisable if ratings are used:

    (1) evaluation by faculty, at least through sampling;
    (2) evaluation by administrative peers:

(3) evaluation by immediate superior;
(4) self-evaluation.

Anyone who has been in the thick of administration readily understands that evaluation must be perceived as a guiding light and not as a critical scoring system. Loyalty should be matched by tolerance, but the same authenticity sought in faculty evaluation is required. Some of the same group principles also may apply.

Much depends on a sense of teamwork (and perhaps a sense of humor) within the administrative group for an exchange to occur. Such a group might use Blake and Mouton's "managerial grid", which rates managers, using a scale of 1 to 9, on concern for production (horizontal scale) and concern for people (vertical scale).[40] Superior managers are those in the 9,9 category. The difficulty of applying this model in an educational institution lies in the difficulty of defining production, though specific goals accomplishment might be used. Concern for people and concern for production are not easily separated where the main product is people. Another group evaluation instrument for administrators is a much more complex form from Likert, which permits greater depth though it is probably less susceptible to group dialogue. Likert defined management models, which he called System 1 and System 4, and developed a profile of organizational characteristics by which a management team could gauge perceptions of where the organization was on the 1 (negative) to 4 (positive) scale.[44] There are other such instruments and games to be borrowed from Organization Development.

As community college administration grows more complex, the administrator needs more management training. The enriching field of Organization Development fulfills this need best. OD administration is not removed from academic concerns in the employment of a quantitative-qualitative matrix. OD projects not an unworkable democracy but shared authority concepts and the primacy of human growth values, such as Maslow, McGregor, *et al*, found at the source of the most effective organizations. (See Chapter Four.)

Faculty are prone to remind administrators that formal evaluation does not always capture the essence of what is going on, and rightly so. Shifting from models to a different kind of analysis, yet with the same purpose in mind, the following section considers a potential nexus of evaluation and aesthetics as taught by John Dewey.

Dewey's Aesthetic Philosophy

The problem of quality does not surrender to scientific, rationalist methods of evaluation, nor does an entirely aesthetic approach achieve an evaluation model. There is need for a heuristic examination of the relationships between quality and quantity in education leading to a greater understanding of why evaluation is not just measurement and how it can be theoretically broadened. In this section and in succeeding chapters, an effort is made to borrow from philosophical works to elucidate this underlying theme. It is an effort to move toward elevating the need for a synthesis, though it is necessarily incomplete. Here the aesthetic philosophy of Dewey is cited as perhaps his most important contribution to education, but no claim is made in these brief comments to a comprehensive treatment.

In considering Dewey's perspective on art, three principles are derived that may be applicable to evaluation in education. Dewey was interested in art because he believed that artistic experience is the paradigm of human experience. For Dewey, art *is* experience. An experience, if it has "unity, pattern, and structure," is an aesthetic experience. Aesthetic experiences are not found in books or art galleries alone. In a community, popular music, parades, celebrations, even newspapers may yield aesthetic experiences. Dewey maintains that aesthetic experience is part and parcel of life on every level.

Citing art, he explains that aesthetic experience is controlled by the conception of the act of making or doing. There is an important distinction between the object which may be thought of as a work of art and the actual work of art, which is that which affects human experience. He explains this distinction through an example of a primitive art object which was found to be a natural product. The object thus ceases to be art; it is merely a curiosity. While there is an element of emotion in all this, a work of art does not evoke only an emotion. It is dependent also on intelligence and past experience. Dewey says that "a work of art is only that when it lives in some individualized experience."[42] A spectator when viewing a painting, for example, must be creative just as the artist was creative. For the artist, it was an experience of organizing his material according to his interest. The spectator must do the same. The painting may "strike" him, but this is merely "an impact that precedes all definition of what it is about."[43] The experience has not yet been fully realized, for discrimination, which may confirm or deny the impact, has not been employed. It follows that, when the spectator has met the artist's interest with his own, the work of art "does not lead to another experience of the world; it *is* an experience."[44]

The first Dewey principle, then — based on the theory that aesthetic experience is not merely an affair of odd moments — is that art, as human experience, is not one of the frills of civilization: it has an "organic place" and must not be segregated. Ignorance of this is one of the reasons for alienation from the arts, an alienation which has contributed to a disorganized technology-intensive society of unfulfilled hopes and possibilities.

Dewey's aesthetic philosophy takes into account several other elements: substance and form, the history of art, the art of artistic expression, criticism, and perception. Their development by Dewey rests on the premise that a work of art, as expressive, is a unique language. The second Dewey principle, then, is that art is a separate medium of communication. The popular view that artistic meaning can be translated into words is one of the barriers between the arts and society. Dewey was hard on critics, whose role, he thought, should not be to judge, for works of art cannot be compared. Seeming to echo Rilke, who said that works of art are of "an infinite loneliness" and cannot be reached by criticism, Dewey felt that the function of the critic was to instruct and so to remove prejudice, thereby revitalizing the connection between art and experience.

In Dewey's philosophical framework, all arts share certain properties. First, they have a common purpose: they are organized toward a unity of experience. Second, they operate through sensory mediums. The medium relates the artist and the spectator. Dewey maintains that "Sensitivity to a medium as a medium is the very heart of all artistic creation and aesthetic perception."[45] In other words, to say that art is a "separate medium of communication" means that it has not one unique language, but several. Third, all arts are connected by the dimensions of space and time. Spaciality is the substance of art; temporality is form. Substance and form are not one, but they are closely related. In the artistic act, there is no distinction: "the act itself is exactly *what* it is because of *how* it is done."[46]

If art is a medium of communication in its own right, it cannot be regarded as a substitute for religion, science, or any other institution. This is not to say, however, that art has no moral function. As Dewey related art, if it is communicative and if it is experience, it has a "moral office and human function," but these can be discussed only in the context of culture:

> The theories that attribute direct moral effect and intent to art fail because they do not take account of the collective civilization that is the context in which works of art are produced and enjoyed. I would not say that they tend to treat works of art as a kind of sublimated Aesop's fables. But, they all tend to extract particular works, regarded as especially edifying, from their milieu and to think of the moral function of art in terms of a strictly personal relation between the selected works and a particular individual. Their whole conception of morals is so individualistic that they miss a sense of the *way* in which art exercises its humane function.[47]

Thus it is possible to draw the final principle. Dewey says, "Just as physical life cannot exist without the support of a physical environment, so moral life cannot go on without the support of a moral environment."[48] It is the function of art to supply this environment without being "moralistic."

The three principles derived from Dewey's aesthetic philosophy are, in sum:

(1) Art is experience; as such, it cannot be isolated.

(2) Art communicates through unique languages.

(3) Art has an important human function: it can serve to create a dynamic, ordered, aesthetic and moral environment.

To interpret is one thing; to apply is another. Assuming that these interpretations are valid, what do they contribute to the evaluation of education?

Aesthetic Connections

There is, first, the evaluation of teaching. When the instructor has his syllabus and lesson plans together, he has a sense of direction. He attempts to formulate certain objectives with the class (which may or may not be stated in behavioral terms) and works toward their achievement. These types of achievement can be measured, and it is important to do so. (By giving exams, for example.) Beyond these objectives, the instructor believes in the value of what he is doing. This value, however, lives in experience. As the instructor and the class relate to the subject matter, they join in an experience. Through this experience, if it has "unity, pattern, and structure," the subject matter takes on meaning which it would not otherwise have if the class were merely plodding ahead, seeking to acquire information or skills.

For example, a history instructor who views his syllabus as an outline of information to be conveyed, and is constantly polishing that same outline, may have objectives, but he is not necessarily experiencing. On the other hand, an instructor who is constantly seeking to organize new materials and striving for a point of view, which he then explains as subject to challenge and change, is more likely to bring to the classroom freshness, spontaneity, and enthusiasm which are infectious. As he interacts with new materials and the class, he is renewed.

How does an instructor motivate a class? If he loses the capacity for approaching the subject matter as an experience, traditional methods of instruction (such as lectures) become boring and ineffective. Out of responsibility, he then attempts to vary the methods knowing that the aesthetic qualities of teaching cannot be faked.[49] He may seek to reconstitute experience by changing the medium. It can be a viable approach if the class begins to interact differently. Success, however, depends upon the ability to handle the medium. Moreover, the relevancy of the subject matter is at stake.

In the cases of both the dynamic and the struggling instructors, the teaching may be judged as effective. If students are the evaluators, they usually are generous toward any instructor who is genuinely interested in their welfare and trying his or her best to create a learning climate. Excellence in teaching, however, depends upon the organization of new materials and sensitivity to the most effective methods of communication. The capacity for new experience — for renewal and growth — is essential to teaching effectiveness. For the creative instructor, the best methods are more easily discovered. For the instructor who has lost the capacity for self-renewal, evaluation tells him that something is wrong, which he probably already knows, though he may be reluctant to admit it. But evaluation, in itself, does not afford him solutions because what he faces is largely an aesthetic problem.

Though now less vigorous, a "fourth revolution" in education began in the 1960s which spread the new doctrine that teachers of the future would be primarily managers of an educational enterprise that relied heavily on teaching machines, computers that talk back, television, and the like. There is no intent here to endorse the Luddite reaction which closed the eyes of some faculty to the potentialities of multimedia instruction. If a given segment of information must be presented in precise terms, there is no reason why an instructor should deliver it five or more times in the same way when it can be more effectively presented on video-tape. Indeed, there are many applications of closed-circuit television, especially, that should be exploited. There also are exciting new ways of creating and using graphic aids, and individualized instruction has been greatly advanced by the use of cassettes. Technology has its place in education.

The assumption that technology would change the fundamental role of the teacher, however, is false. Technology makes teaching a science, whereas teaching has always been primarily an art. As an art, it is sometimes difficult to judge why it is effective or ineffective because, obliquely, the effects are felt just from the "being there" of the teacher who knows his or her task. A machine can never substitute for the human presence in genuine educational relationships. There are faculty who are gifted discussion leaders. But there are others who use the straight lecture method (frowned upon by most evaluation specialists), yet students love them. Why? The heuristics of this question may be promoted by adding to the investigations of behavioral science, the philosophy of aesthetics.

The College Environment/Community

The third principle derived from Dewey's philosophy — that of the creation of an aesthetic environment — illustrates the values of the arts and philosophy in the college curricula if there is dynamic mission involvement. Apart from the question of applying aesthetics, however, environmental considerations require an analytic framework.

By a general systems approach, the environment is a composite of systems within which the college system exists. By another organic model, the college may be seen as a community which relates to the larger community it serves. One model does not invalidate the other. Both are useful. In formal evaluation, there are instruments available for measuring the general health of the college's immediate environment (that is, the internal effects of the organization's energy and resources exploitation.)[50]

Looking at the problem of community, however, moves the discussion out of the context of formal evaluation. The community model is particularly appropriate for discussing in a practical way some other growing concerns of the community college. Among these concerns is the control of conflict. As conflict grows more intense in society, the challenge of modeling the college as a community and finding ways to handle conflict grows as well. The next chapter deals with this challenge.

Summary

Formal evaluation requires a systematic approach combining quantitative information with qualitative judgment. Though many different approaches are possible, successful implementation depends upon clear models. First to be modeled is a Management Information System developed according to the college's needs. Six MIS categories are suggested: statistical, student research, financial and budgeting, college environment, community and work-force research, and facilities usage. The first three categories are becoming increasingly important for accountability. MIS development is seen as primarily a social problem. Accountability has led to a concern about productivity and cost-analysis. Cost-simulation models assist in cost analysis. Strongly disputed is the notion of measuring cost-effectiveness in an educational institution: the quality problem does not surrender to quantitative approaches. Qualitative analysis is the aim of a model which dovetails individual evaluation, group evaluation, and programs evaluation. A consultation model for programs evaluation and criteria for assessing program priorities are outlined. The major points raised with regard to faculty evaluation are: (1) individual evaluation should be emphasized but with flexible provisions for its conduct, including student ratings; (2) the vitality of the evaluation process depends upon group dynamics. The group is seen as the basic change unit in the organization. Organization Development strategies are suggested. Emphasis is shifted from practical administration to philosophy. Dewey's aesthetic philosophy is tied to examination of the quality problem. Three aesthetic principles are derived. In applying aesthetics to evaluation, the capacity for self-renewal — particularly through experiencing the subject matter — is seen as the most essential ingredient for effective teaching. Attention is turned to community and conflict.

COMMUNITY AND CONFLICT

A cross-sectional reading of community college catalogs reveals their common philosophical concern for the individual and for community. In its most ideal form, then, the community college strives for "maximum individuality within maximum community." (Kant) The problem is that, whereas a symbiosis of these values is possible and has been achieved by many colleges, particularly in early stages of development, its maintenance over time is not possible without change; yet change is also the enemy. Change is necessary not for the sake of instilling values, but to allow the organization to remain effective. Without demonstrated effectiveness (accountability), the organization cannot cope with its environment. Organizational effectiveness (goals accomplishment), therefore, is a life force. Coming full circle, however, organizational effectiveness depends upon how well the organization serves and is served by those basic values which form a large part of the justification for its existence.

In community colleges today, it is the concept of community which is most threatened. As humans are social beings, where community is lost, individuality also suffers. Thus, as difficult as it is to assess the interdependence of individuality and community, it is important to not separate these values in discussion. They must be defined, of course, but in a systems context rather than according to a reductionist view.

Community Within Community

Community is the opposite of alienation, aloneness, non-alliance, impersonal action. Communities of various types are constantly struggling to be born. While a sense of integrity is imbued in the notion of a community, individuals do not identify with one community exclusively. Thus, a religious community may form alongside a political community within the same geographical area. A college may be seen as part of a larger academic community; yet, in the sense of serving as an educational model, which is the challenge of the community college, it should more nearly approximate what Nisbet has defined as the *plural* community: it derives the "all-important idea of *communitas communitatum*, community of communities."[51] More precisely, in this sense, it serves the idea that diversity, autonomy, and decentralization still are possible for local communities, coexisting and co-supporting, within the larger community. As a philosophical concept, *community* does not necessarily imply localism, though, as Nisbet also has pointed out, localism is a strong element in the notion of a pluralistic community.

Does not this emphasis on localism invite those provincial attitudes which we have already seen as the main threat to educational vitality? Only if the college fails to serve as a model community, for it is by the example of its outward reaching for new ideas, for sharing, and for mediating that the college gives claim to itself as a pluralistic community.

As the college is seen as a community interacting with other communities, its roles and identity are shaped more clearly. It is not a governmental agency or department which dispenses services in a manner similar to that of a civil service bureau. Services flowing from a community model are legitimate only to the extent that they are an extension or expansion of the educational missions of the college. The college's educational role in community development springs naturally from its own relative developmental strength. Among those functions which are common to both internal and external developmental perspectives are organization development assistance, analysis of community problems, discussion of group concerns and group interactions, and provision of opportunities for greater self-awareness through cultural and recreational activities and skills training. The college operates as a forum and a center for diverse activities while providing educational programs and perhaps coordination which reflect a pluralistic community. By avoiding both bureaucratic stereotypy and amorphousness, the values of community are maintained.

The college is a community in microcosm. All of the same problems of growth and conflict, political and moral issues, and the like, which are present in the larger community exist within the college community. It even may be construed as a laboratory for "experimental living" (Becker) if connections are made between college life and those theories and principles which are addressed in its classrooms. To a large degree, the relevance of what goes on in the classroom is lessened if the model potential is not seen. Stated in another way, if the problem of community is not specifically and continually addressed by the college in its own terms, how can it be expected that community life somehow is fostered elsewhere?

Attention to the community model does not mean physical containment, however. Few community colleges have been built as ivory towers. Pluralism means making connections with a variety of outside groups through off-campus efforts. As needs are discovered, a continual assessment of priorities based upon the inventory of resources is required. What interests and expertise of the professional staff can be tapped? What physical properties off campus can be utilized? What community groups and individuals can be enlisted for programs and activities that can be coordinated and managed appropriately? These are questions germane to the planning process. In this process, an opportunity is presented for strengthening external relationships, but the college needs to know how to refuse those invitations and demands which would undermine its integrity or which are beyond its resources capability. In doing so, it is further educating as to what community is. (By the same token, occasionally it may need to resist general judgments by peer evaluators as to what it should be doing.)

Obviously, to serve as a model means first to set one's own community in order. If the college does not emanate qualities of mutual respect and support (synergy) among its own people and a steady development despite the accompanying tensions and conflict, it hardly will earn the respect of those outside groups bearing witness to its influence. With this in mind, a deeper understanding of the problem of community is required. What combinations of forces and concepts contribute to community development? What causes its regression?

There are numerous sources which are helpful in this analysis though they do not necessarily afford direct aid in the quest for community. The daily, pragmatic search for applications goes on beyond theory. The experienced administrator learns to hold the theories he encounters in abeyance and to look around instead, searching for that combination which makes the most sense and seems to have durability. Theorists may find fault with this eclecticism, but strict adherence to any single theory or doctrine usually reaps much greater fault for the administration. Whatever the right combination is, it is never revealed to administration alone, nor is it solely an administrative concern. When this point of limited knowledge and responsibility in any single group or individual within the organization begins to internalize, the chances of community development are probably raised significantly.

Administration carries leadership obligations, of course, the foremost of which is motivation. Since administration is always in need of shoring up its motivational strategies and techniques, the coexistence with theory must continue. In the following treatment, a three-dimensional approach is taken: community development first is seen as a matter of fostering organizational health through humanistic psychology (for which the debt to Maslow is great indeed), then as a problem of conflict-resolution, and finally, as a recognition of transformational principles of growth in which community is isomorphic with nature. Since the modeling aim is the community college, the discussion of "community development" is tempered accordingly.

Theories X, Y, B and D

This section examines the human behavior theories of McGregor and Maslow. McGregor's "Y Theory" and "Eupsychian management" as outlined by Maslow are virtually synonymous. These theories underlie both the MBO and "natural systems" practical approaches to administration which were discussed in Chapter Two."[52] Thus, through an examination of theoretical underpinnings, the good end of administration (to wit, strengthening of community) is elevated higher than in the discussion of styles, strategy, and the like. On the action level, however, interpretations and the social dynamics of application may enter quite different roads though starting from a similar vision of ends. The objective here is not to compare administrative models but to sketch a deliberately chosen theoretical framework because it helps to illuminate the basic values under consideration.

This framework begins with McGregor's work on leadership. McGregor saw the traditional view of management direction and control (which he labeled *Theory X*) as based on deeply-rooted assumptions about human nature and behavior (for example, the average person dislikes work, wants security above all, prefers to be directed) which call for authoritarian, hierarchical administration. Motivation in this mode is of the "carrot-and-stick" variety. New strategies aimed at decentralizing authority usually fail because procedures used to implement them "are derived from the same inadequate assumptions about human nature."[53] McGregor echoes Maslow's description of the hierarchy of needs[54] and proceeds from this line of humanistic interpretation to *Theory Y*, which is based essentially on an opposite set of assumptions (that is, work may be a source of satisfaction; creativity, self-direction, and sense of responsibility are natural in most people.)

Since self-motivation is seen as a strong innate potential, waiting to be released, the task of leadership is to build a commitment to excellence by properly challenging the abilities and interests of people within the organization.

Theory Y differs most from Theory X in its emphasis on *integration* as the central principle of organization. Integration demands that both the organization's needs and the individual's needs be recognized in any decision-making process and, further, that the individual should be an active participant in the total needs assessment. It follows that Theory Y management is straightforward and open to influence, facing realistically the problem of integrating the individual and the organization if for no other reason than that organizational effectiveness depends upon it. (Maslow readily came to share this view.)

McGregor's Theory Y first was presented in 1960. Since then, a number of other management studies have reinforced its efficacy for modern corporations, and a considerable amount of Organization Development literature can be traced to it. There is nothing new about these management principles today except that integration can be seen not just as a means for improving individual work situations and productivity but as a vital means for community development. What McGregor called "integration" can be discussed more fully in the systems context as *synergy*. Before examining this context, however, much can be gained from Maslow's theories of motivation and self-actualization to sharpen this view.

Maslow described Values of Being (B-values) and Value-deficiencies (D-values). The former include not only those classical philosophic aims of truth, goodness, and beauty but also a range of Eupsychian management values, such as integration, openness, trust, and meaningfulness. (Maslow cited about 14 such values, also calling them "meta-needs".) D-values are their opposites — disintegration distrust, discouragement, disbelief, despair. According to Maslow, B-values are intrinsic and "are instinctoid in nature, i.e., they are needed (a) to avoid illness and (b) to achieve fullest humanness or growth."[55] Such a statement, of course, is revolutionary in the social sciences.

Maslow made these values a proper subject of scientific study and research.[56] Some of his empirical work would seem difficult to replicate by any less astute, less self-actualized researchers, and Maslow lamented in his last writings that more research was not being done. There can be no question, however, that humanistic psychology (including Eupsychian management) is now an established, vibrantly important field of knowledge which has freed social science from the positivistic stranglehold and is changing fundamentally our ways of thinking about individuals, groups, and community. It is now possible to speak of "spiritual values" without losing rationalist credentials or being accused of fuzzy-headed idealism. Indeed, in theoretical consideration, there is no more tough-minded position to be taken than a rationalist, naturalistic approach to valuation, though it may not be complete.

What is most interesting to the administrator is the enthusiastic recognition in Maslow's work, from at least 1965 on, that B-values and B-cognition applied equally in theories of management and organization. This is primarily because Eupsychian conditions of work are good not only for personal fulfillment but are the best guarantee of the health and prosperity of the organization. The theories of McGregor and Maslow are not sufficient, however, for a theory-action marriage in administration. Organization Development recognizes this insufficiency. New applications must be sought continually while at the same time fostering management control through MIS development. Such a balance will not be achieved easily. Indeed, it seems hardly possible at all without reaffirming the values base.

The OD administrator's debt to McGregor and Maslow is for their revelation of those values which motivate self-actualizing individuals (more matured, more fully human).[57] It follows that, in any institution which claims as its basic purpose the development of individuals to their fullest capacity (the most desirable kind of "productivity"), the most effective organization is one which strives to incorporate these theories.

Organization Health and Synergy

The community college is a fertile ground for an effort in Maslow's direction; but, at the same time, it should be recognized that a college is no more laden with B-values over D-values than is an industrial work organization. Maslow was clear as to the tensions which exist. The truth of the newer system of values includes a dichotomy in human behavior which repels as well as motivates. In other words, the individual desires truth, but he is also afraid of truth. He seeks beauty, yet he is confused about what it is. Theory Y or Eupsychian management capitalizes on the B-values; indeed, it does not work in a D-values context. According to Maslow, there is a reciprocal relationship between healthy people and Theory Y, and, conversely, the same kind of reciprocal relationship between unhealthy people and Theory X. "To trust paranoics is a very foolish thing."[58]

If Theory Y works best with healthy people, one might suppose that the task is to count up the number of healthy people in the organization. Facile suggestions of this sort are useless, however. Apart from the problem of agreeing on a definition of "health" and making judgments, they fail because the organization is not only a composite of healthy and/or unhealthy individuals. In regard to organization, the most feasible approach would appear to be an ongoing effort to assess the positive versus the regressive forces which influence groups. A positive balance holds good promise for Eupsychian management. A negative balance would require reversion to the older authoritarian structure in the interest of survival. While this assessment also is difficult and might result only in neutrality, at least it confronts the question of organization health.

What is "organization health"? And what are the regressive forces?

Criteria of organization health, based on facsimile of healthy personality, are offered by Bennis:[59]

1. Adaptability — problem-solving ability; freedom to learn through experience, to change with changing internal and external requirements.

2. Identity — to develop adaptability, the organization needs to know what it is and what it is to do. (To what extent are the organization goals understood and accepted by its personnel?)

3. Reality-testing — adequate techniques for determining the "real properties" of the field in which it exists.

This systems view is in line with the theories of McGregor and Maslow. The concept of *synergy* can be added to the definition. Synergy establishes the connection between organization health and community development. A sense of community does not necessarily result because the organization is healthy, but a sense of community cannot develop if the organization is sick. Synergy promotes a positive spirit which flows into community endeavor.

With respect to community, the McGregor and Maslow theories lead inescapably to the conclusion that, far from being in opposition, community and individuality are inextricably related and are mutually dependent on organization health. Individuals and groups within the organization have certain self-interests, which might as well be labeled "selfishness," and it is unrealistic to expect that this selfishness can be repressed. However, selfishness moves on a continuum of unhealthy narrowness and ignorance to enlightened self-interest or being "healthily selfish." (Fromm) Self-actualizing people more readily understand the degrees of difference and therefore are better able to resolve their conflict. They know what "synergy" means.

Synergy stresses the interdependence of individuals within the group and of groups within the organization. A synergic institution is one in which it truly can be said that the advancement of group interests contributes to greater institutional effectiveness and vice-versa. (What's good for the faculty is good for the college, and what's good for the college is good for the faculty.) Attempts to steer competing demands toward greater compatability and flexibility in problem-solving are a reflection of synergic relationships. Inability to distinguish value sets or acceptance of the mutual exclusiveness of self-interests and community interests are signs of a lack of synergy. It is expressed in the quality and the rate of interactions.

The higher the rate of interactions between individuals and groups, the more likely it is that loyalty and teamwork will emerge.[60] Perhaps an example of these synergic tendencies is seen in a good professional hockey team which consciously relies on teamwork and yet, within which each player performs as an individual. Such individuality is expressed not only by the number of shots on goal a player makes but, even more, by his ability to move the puck and get it to his team-mates. The individual scoring system counts assists equally with goals.

There are also two other features in this example which imply something about synergy. The best hockey team does not win all the time. There are winning qualities in the game that cannot be captured by formula. On a given night, the league-leading team may lose to a "cellar" team. The loss is accepted; it does not destroy confidence. Nor do players and coaches normally discuss such losses as a matter of "bad luck." Turns were made that simply did not pay off, or, for no apparent reason, players made mistakes that they did not make on other nights. As one coach put it, "Teams do not play the same all the time. It's not like pushing the button on a machine and having it operate at the same tempo."

Synergy, in other words, is a fluid pattern of relationships that raises the probability of things moving well, but it does not assure perfection.

Conflict does not disappear. To use the hockey team example, in one publicized case of personal conflict between two team-mates, one was asked if the dispute would affect his passing the puck to the other. His immediate answer demonstrates synergy: "Do you think I'm stupid? If I don't pass him the puck, I don't play well. Do you think I want to hurt my game?" Granted, this example is not entirely representative: professional sports and combat games are not equivalent to the complexities of community life. But the demonstration of synergistic principles is valid nonetheless.

Part of the problem of communicating synergistic principles in the college is a kind of group ethnocentricity: trustees, administrators, faculty, and students are apt to feel that the college belongs to or at least depends primarily on them ("the faculty are the college" . . . "the college exists for students" . . . "without us, the college would fall apart," and so on.) These perspectives are not unhealthy, just incomplete. It is difficult to achieve a perspective of the organized complexity of institutional "belongingness," which is what synergy is.

But why should synergy be singled out from those qualities that fit a definition of *organization health*? Because the community college organization has so much to do with community. The argument has already been presented that the college's strength within the community (and, thereby, its support) is related to its strength *as* a community. A hypothesis is that one of the college's future main lines of development shall lie in the establishment of educational community services which require professional staff cooperation well beyond that required to introduce new courses. Community-based services and programs require rapid administrative orientation to the knowledge needs and good support relationships among faculty of different disciplinary backgrounds. A math unit, for example, may be needed as part of a larger program which cannot wait for six months of curriculum processing. Still, the math faculty must be concerned about the integrity of math offerings. The maintenance of this integrity will depend on faith in professional relationships within the community model which are best described as "synergic." Moreover, a synergic base is essential for the development of general education. (This topic is discussed at length in Chapter Six.)

Regression and Conflict

It would be a mistake to confuse organization health with such ideals as happiness and contentment. Early human relations efforts in management failed badly because of such confusion. By the nature of organization, tension and conflict will exist. As Maslow said, "Conflict is, of course, a sign of relative health as you would know if you ever met really apathetic people, people who have given up hoping, striving and coping."[61] In those terms, each group is responsible for its own morale. Just as the individual must look to God for salvation, and not to other men, so the continual satisfaction of all groups is not possible by any organizational means and should not be assumed as an obligation. (Maslow's "Grumble theory" shows its impossibility very well.) This parameter does not imply that good will is of little value or that there is no obligation to strive for rapport. As the congruities of peace are infinitely preferable to the comradeship of wartime, congenial relations between groups, as well as within groups, are much to be desired and can be achieved. But they need not be present initially to foster growth and collaboration.

What prevents positive growth and collaboration are the same regressive forces that, when dominant, would make Theory Y or Eupsychian management a mockery. Within the organization, a constant struggle is going on between growth and regression (almost dialectical, but the dialectical method is not a good one for understanding qualitative issues). On both sides, there are activists and quiet types, doers and complainers of several types (for example, doers who complain and doers who do not complain), innovators and traditionalists, conservatives and radicals, and so forth. There have been many efforts to categorize faculty and administrator types, most of which have not gotten very far. Attendance at any group meeting in which the dialogue degenerates to left/right ideology ("Are you a radical or not?") shows the uselessness of this approach for getting a handle on the struggle.

Growth is defined in the section which follows as a "unifying principle of transformation." (Land) *Regression* is the avoidance of, or moving away from, growth patterns, usually because of fear and insecurity. It is important to note that a philosophical argument against a planned change effort does not fit this definition. (On the contrary, if it is honestly worked up, it is a sign of growth!) If it is healthy, the organization always is in a growth position, but it also strives for adaptation. As with cancerous cells in the body, too much growth would be harmful.

Other conditions which cause regression are perceptual distortion and a lack of communications, dishonesty in evaluation, and a scarcity of resources. A combination of these conditions over time could bring about fear of responsibility and hesitation to participate in decision-making. Conflict may be deliberately muted: That is, a state of apathy may be induced. Since a vacuum is not created, however, this regression demands more centralized authority. The emerging D-values preclude Eupsychian management. As the situation moves from bad to worse, conflict is likely to occur again, of a more virulent type — less susceptible to mediation and more easily escalated through threat and counter-threat. M. Deutsch's studies on conflict demonstrated that tactics of threat, coercion, and deception resulted in increased competitiveness.[62] The use of threat is effective only if immediate punitive power exists to carry it out.

Maslow's focus on studying healthy people led him to the conclusion that negative feelings, such as guilt, sorrow, and shame, are normal in healthy people and may become motivational in a self-actualizing way. Moreover, motivations find many different channels. Exemplifying this in another way, Fromm described the differences between benign and malignant incestuousness, the latter being one of the roots of necrophilia, but the former being a normal, transitory stage of development.[63] Applying this knowledge to an assessment of organization health, there are two points to keep in mind: (1) there are bound to be some regressive tendencies in any organization; and (2) regression is not non-growth. In other words, some regression is normal, but too much of it does not signal a static condition. Rather, it produces an unhealthy kind of growth, manifested in the destructive variety of conflict and an increase in pathologies (which can ultimately lead to a static condition called ''death''). The ineluctability of growth in some form is examined further in the concluding section.

Conflict-Resolution

Clearly, both positive growth and regression lead to conflict (more precisely, they are cyclical). So, just as clearly, there are considerable differences in the nature of the conflict, depending upon the environmental sources. In his general theory of conflict, Boulding observes:

> In any given social situation or sub-system, we can perhaps postulate an optimum amount or degree of conflict. The concept is hard to specify, but it is of great importance. It relieves us immediately, for instance, from the illusion that conflict in any amount is either good or bad in itself. The evaluation of conflict has two aspects: quantitative and qualitative. In any given situation, we may have too much or too

> little conflict, or the amount may be just right. There is no
> simple operational definition of such an optimum; we must
> rely for our information on a complex structure of attitudes
> and evaluations. In a given situation, we may also have the
> wrong kind of conflict. Here again, there is no simple opera-
> tional definition, but common speech has words that de-
> scribe these qualitative differences: conflicts may be bitter
> and destructive or they may be fruitful and constructive.[64]

Applying Boulding's statement to the community college environment, the measurement of the level of conflict, or even the assessment
of conditions leading to it, is not likely to be gained from institutional
research. Indicators are possible through various attitudinal surveys,
but the quantitative and qualitative aspects of conflict and conflict-
resolution may be monitored more effectively through dialogue among
influential group representatives and leaders. Influence-mapping is a
part of this process. What is suggested here is not T-Group training nor
that dialogue which goes on as issues are raised, as in collective
bargaining or contract administration. Instead, what is proposed is an
objective removal from the scene of the immediate issues to a higher
level of B-value considerations. (How are we doing, and how does it
look for the long haul?)

Since no one is free from the pressures and biases generated by
conflict, there is no point in pretending wisdom or superior objectivity
about it. Such dialogue, however, would have to relate to other concepts, such as community and professional development. The difficulty, of course, is that each group sees the organization differently
because of uneven experiencing. What seems healthy to one faction
may be unhealthy to another. Similarly, what seems like apathy and
non-involvement may be countered by what seems like too much
pressure.[65] If these beliefs are not scrutinized, they remain hanging in the
atmosphere, clouding perspectives further, and reducing the hopes for
future collaboration even on mutually held self-interests. Admonitions
such as, "Let's be more mature about it" usually do not help. As
Maslow suggests, it is probably better just to assume maturity, self-
actualization, and good will. In the future, perceptual differences could
grow even more acute if group interactions (for example, between
faculty and administration) decrease as a result of formalized arrangements. What is suggested, therefore, is a form of intellectual discourse
on this general problem as it affects the college.

Here, then, is one form of communication, but not sufficient by itself. If it is true that the higher the rate of interactions, the greater the chance for developing synergic relationships, then obviously several modes of communication must be established. Communication facilitators are needed in all groups. Equally needed are those mature personalities who may be counted upon to provide informal mediation efforts as serious disputes erupt. They need not be directly involved in the disputes at the beginning but are enlisted or choose to become involved because of what they see as overriding issues. These leaders are not "appointed"; they are just there. Since conflict has its origins in a complex matrix of interests, so that it is not easy to detect until it has erupted, it is difficult to estimate how much conflict is resolved into growth patterns as a result of non-authority, self-actualizing influence. The amount is probably far greater than the conflict resolved by administrative authority, or, at least, it would be in a synergic institution.

Conflict should not be avoided when real issues arise.[66] The resolution is likely to be more successful if the "day of battle" is not postponed for too long. Avoidance may be one way to end a dispute, but as we have seen, hostilities grow. Early resolution attempts should be made on a level where the issues are most immediate. It is a serious management error — and a symptom of poor organization health — to rush all issues to the highest level for conflict-resolution or to wait for such intercession. This is not to suggest that top administrators should dodge internal politics, but, since they are neither omniscient nor omnipotent, their presence is not always good.

There are numerous methods for resolving conflict, but three seem to predominate: (1) arbitration — after hearing all parties and weighing the evidence, a decision is made; (2) compromise — all parties relinquish something in order to move off dead center; and (3) reconciliation — the parties are joined so that the same value position is held by all. (Arbitration is discussed in relation to collective bargaining; see Chapter Five.) Compromise is a typical way out of conflict. Blake and Mouton contend that it is not an acceptable course by superior standards of management because it is always a "sell-out of principles." This argument, however, seems overdrawn; at times, there is no other way to break a deadlock in which equal merits exist on both sides. Thus, compromise may be called a low form of successful mediation.

The highest form of mediation would resolve the conflict not only by reconciling the parties but in such a way that the result contributes to the organization as well. To achieve this may mean that one of the parties must bend substantially on its position. If so, the reconciliation would come out of respect for the organization's best interests, returned in full measure by respect for the dignity of the losing party. The mediator(s) should seek from the beginning to depersonalize the issues. Too, out of the dialogue, a completely new position might have to be formed which the parties agree has greater quality than that of either of the original positions which were in conflict. In mediation, the controlling factor always should be a concern for qualitative growth.

In a steady state, most issues revolve around the theme of qualitative rather than quantitative growth. Program or enrollment retrenchment resulting in loss of people could stimulate vulgarization of the growth theme, further compounding the analytic difficulties. It seems important, therefore, to arrive at a better understanding of the growth process.

Growth and Adaptation

There is much said about the "quality of life" and the need to bring technology under the service of this all-inclusive concept. But, as we have seen, "quality" is difficult to define. What is it that we mean by "quality of life" other than a yearning for general improvement of society and the environment and a hope that the demonic forces threatening their existence can be stopped somehow? Quality is approached primarily through aesthetics, which is why aesthetic experience is so important to community life. Dewey's vision of an environment created and ordered by art is exemplary of this approach. (See Chapter Three.) What Dewey saw, of course, was not a fixed Utopian model but an experiential model for qualitative growth.

There may be another way of getting at qualitative growth: through acceptance of a general systems view of the comparability of growth processes in biological and social organisms. There is, first, the naturalistic view that man, as a being in nature, is subject to the same processes as the rest of the biological world, even accounting for his difference in kind. What is more disputed by social scientists is the parallel view that social organizations are growth-oriented in the same way as biological organisms are. (This does not mean that the comparisons are not true, of course; it merely means that they are not yet satisfactorily proven.) A contribution to this view is made through general systems theory by George T. Lock Land.

In describing the "unifying principle of transformation," Lock Land presents the thesis that all life forms share the same behavioral processes. These processes are focused on growth. *Growth* is defined as "a continual joining of larger amounts of information (energy) into meaningful relationships, in an organized form."[67] There are three types of growth: (1) accretive — enlargement of the total organism, which is merely additive and identical; (2) replicative — growth through generation of other like organisms or the development of affiliative relationships in which the growth of each organism is reinforced; and (3) mutual — growth through symbiotic relationships, which, even though complex, are characterized by a high degree of cooperation between *different* organisms attracted to each other for mutual growth support. All systems tend to evolve by progressing from one level to the next, always as a result of environmental interactions and relations.

Through a series of examples, Land demonstrates growth in psychological and social systems as well as in physical and biological systems through the same principles. The conclusion is that living processes are ubiquitous and universal: "Transformation maintains that psychological and cultural processes are an extension of and are isomorphic with biological, physical, and chemical processes."[68]

How does this work further our understanding of organization and community development? In fostering the community concept, quality is the general aim, but the creation of environmental conditions which allow intrinsic values (for example, Maslow's B-values) has more social science direction. In this sense, what helps directly, at least in understanding the growth problem, is the application of transformational principles in a circumscribed area. Land explains community growth, for example, as most healthful when it has achieved a stage of "mutualism," that is, when physical growth is accompanied by the equal growth of communication patterns, good support systems, relationships with other communities, and so forth. The community as an organism remains autonomous but not isolated. When the continued physical growth occurs, however, as a "new form of accretive," a pathological state may be created in which the community's functions break down under too much pressure. As Land states:

> The pathology of extending accretive growth is easily detected in many closed or self-isolated systems; the monolithic organizations of today — public utilities, churches, multiversities — serve as excellent examples as they also find that bigger is not better. Imposition of increasingly stringent controls, rules, and standards to protect and

to maintain accretive growth does not work. In fact, it does just the opposite, for closing a system to new alternatives inevitably results in either radical changes or collapse and extinction.[69]

Land's analysis clearly implies principles of adaptation as well as of growth in the transformational process. For an understanding of the place and meaning of adaptation, Laszlo's explanation is more helpful. It strengthens the previously expressed view that the relationships between any system and its environment are dynamically worked out as the system strives to fit itself well into its environment and to make the environment fit its needs at the same time. Laszlo provides an example quite relevant to the purpose of this discussion:

> Adaptation often requires the restructuring of some part of the environment, as a precondition of achieving more complete adaptation to the whole environment. If a university is alienated from the rest of society, for example, through offering outdated programs and a restrictive general learning environment, it imposes alienation on all faculty, students and staff who accept its standards. These individuals will find themselves maladapted to the larger society within which the university functions. It is therefore in the interest of all members of such an institution to make their institution well adapted to contemporary society on all its multiple levels. Only by so doing can their own social adaptation to the institution signify adaptation to society in a wider context.[70]

If truth is ascribed to these principles, the gleanings from humanistic psychology and conflict theory are reinforced. Everything comes together. Growth should no longer be seen as an expanding process only. That "bigger is not better" certainly applies to the need for curtailing centralizing tendencies in higher education and the dependency on more and more resources. A larger economic pie does not necessarily lead to quality of growth; and, in fact, colleges may discover that quality is enhanced by steady-state economics if attention is turned to the intrinsic values in healthy conflict. For such a future to unfold, however, a values shift must occur.

In Chapter Five, reference is made to the issues of constricting resources and the closing of the extrinsic rewards system in community colleges. What are the possibilities of sustaining qualitative growth under such conditions? Are they not tied essentially to a more enlightened view of "mutualism" and of synergy in community development? The vicissitudes of individual and group development are too great for any planning doctrine apart from community.

The average community college educator probably has 25 or more years of service ahead. How shall these years be spent? What are the B-values? There is no particular justification for granting significantly higher economic rewards to some professional staff members simply because they came on board a few years earlier than others, who may have surpassed them in contributions; but, whether this question of justice is resolved or left unresolved, economic rewards are neither valid nor reliable for motivation in the future and must be supplanted by commonly-held intrinsic rewards.

As Maslow demonstrates in his psychology of Being, a mature B-cognitive perspective on the need for growth is not the same as the older, competitive view that one always should be striving for something higher, something missing. Being, rather than becoming, is a trait of self-actualization. A mature growth perspective does recognize the validity of intrinsic rewards in professional work. Individuality in this perspective is tied closely to the idea of work as a reward in itself. As Maslow states. "[Self-actualizing] individuals assimilate their work into their identity, into the self, i.e., work actually becomes part of the self, part of the individual's definition of himself."[71]

Again, it is easy to state the case for intrinsic values, but the social shift is difficult. The history of community college development has been made by climbers. To not climb has social risks. (The "Peter principle" is still in vogue.) Assistant professors are supposed to become associate professors, department chairmen are supposed to become deans, deans to become presidents, and so it has gone. Mobility will not disappear altogether (nor does this infer that department chairmen should not become deans), but the unfolding picture of a steady state clearly implies the need for a different model. The plain facts of the socio-economic situation demand it, and the social future is likely to achieve it with or without comfort to the current players. A new model can grow out of the world view which has brought human potential development front and center, a movement introducing new concepts of power and progress aimed not at quick achievement but at balanced life.

Thus, the basic values of individuality and community upon which the community college was founded are even more valid and worthy of commitment. Moreover, the community college enjoys an excellent position in higher education for exercising leadership in the continued advancement of these values through general education. (See Chapter Six.) The fostering of these values depends upon the mature under-standing and allegiance of the full-time professional staff, whose concerns and responsibilities extend well beyond the classroom. Good teaching can be maintained by part-time instructors as well as by the full-time faculty, but it is the latter who give meaning and life to the college as something greater than a training institute. If the professional staff can hold on to a vision of the community in the community college, despite new storms, this positive picture can be made reality.

A serious question now intrudes, however, upon the possibilities of maintaining the commitment to community in the future. What will be the impact of collective bargaining? So far, in this analysis, there has been an assumption that shared authority concepts are possible and desirable. The assumption now must be questioned from another vantage point. The next chapter examines the impact of collective bargaining.

Summary

The enlightenment ideal phrased by Kant — "maximum individuality within maximum community" — is seen as the philosophical bedrock of the community college. The view of the college as a pluralistic community is set forth, while recognizing that the community concept is under duress, therefore requiring a deeper understanding of those forces which promote or hinder community development. Linking the development of a sense of community to the state of organization health, the theories of McGregor and Maslow are explored. McGregor's Theory Y emphasis on integrating individual needs and the organization needs corresponds with Maslow's description of Eupsychian management values (B-values). In attempting to define organization health, reference is made to the importance of synergy, that is, the interdependence of individuals and groups within the organization. Individuals and groups have their own self-interests and perceptual differences, thereby leading to conflict. Self-actualizing individuals are better able to understand and mediate conflict, which takes both constructive and destructive forms. The destructive form is traced to the dominance of regressive forces, which also preclude the success of Eupsychian management. In a steady-state environment, conflict-resolution becomes increasingly important as a means of maintaining growth which is qualitative rather than quantitative. *Growth* is defined according to principles of transformation, which hold that community growth is isomorphic with all other growth in nature. In conclusion about the need for a mature perspective on growth, which heightens awareness of the intrinsic rewards, Maslow again is cited on self-actualization. Attention is turned to collective bargaining.

V

THE IMPACT OF COLLECTIVE BARGAINING

What chance does a shared-authority model have in the future of collective bargaining on the community college campus? Faculty union ideologists claim that it just will be born. They speak of unionism on campus as the force of academic democracy (without seeing that majoritarian rule and shared authority are not the same thing). Some trustees and administrators who have experienced the travail of collective bargaining and have witnessed the debilitating effects of its crises see the end of traditional concepts of college governance. The tide is strong for a corporate management model. Militant unionists contend that colleges already are run like corporations. Both camps are saying, in effect: "Collegiality is dead. Long live the contract!" Middle-grounders are accused of clinging to romantic fallacies that merely prolong the aggravation in moving to the new order. College administrators and faculty leaders caught in such a vise become constrained in their valor, if it is such, to press for adaptation rather than for wholesale change. What follows is a middle-ground view.

While recognizing the uncertainty of the outcome as collective bargaining gathers momentum, there is still a need for considering the traditional values of education and their juxtaposition to the new, controlling emphases of industrial change. The tradition in these values is not the contemporary assignation of old things for the sake of the old, but a facsimile of that definition which comes to us from Oppenheimer:

> Tradition, of course, is to preserve, to refresh, to transmit, and to increase our insight into what men have done as men, in their art, their learning, their poetry, their religion, their politics, their science. Feeling, thinking beings, with our experiences, to cope with our sorrows, to limit and make noble our joys, to understand what is happening to us, to talk to one another, to relate one thing to another, to find the great themes which organize our experience and give it meaning — it is what makes us human.[72]

Behind the need to find an effective approach to collective bargaining is the greater need to build a governance system which not only adjusts to the reality of a union on campus but which continues to advance the educational purposes of the college as a teaching institution. Collective bargaining may contribute to this greater need. Or, it may not. If it does not, it is clear that the college will not retain its traditional role. Whatever it is to become, it will have a different identity. To say that institutional integrity is at stake is not an alarmist view. When collective bargaining appears, to view the situation otherwise, is to miss the significance of its potential impact.

In the community college sector, at least, collective bargaining seems here to stay. It is possible, of course, that some community colleges may opt to not go this route. In such cases, it is likely that the collegial systems and the processes which serve the faculty's vested interests are so well developed as to enable the faculty of these colleges to resist the pull of unionization. Some faculties have voted to reject all agents, but these declinations seem to be more a putting off the fateful step than a final resolution of choice. The 1975 Ladd-Lipset survey reported that 81 per cent of all two-year college faculty respondents were in favor of a bargaining agent.[73] Given this level of expressed support, it is fantasy to assume that the tide can be reversed. Attention must turn to the problem of balancing the effects.

Defining the Model

Collective bargaining is perhaps the most humorless subject in the array of community college governance concerns. Tension, suspicion, distrust, irrationality, and ideological extremism — all these draining properties of conflict — seem to coalesce easily at one or several points in the bargaining process. Since collective bargaining also is the newest feature of college governance, it may be for this reason that experience of it seems to be so raw.[74]

At the outset, colleges are not attuned to the mechanics of the collective-bargaining process and lack the tools for reducing the behavioral disturbance. Psychological unreadiness, in the form of uncertainty about procedures, legal implications, and demand expectations, creates a polarization of the parties that looms larger than the vital issues separating them in the contract to be achieved. There are hidden agendas and underlying issues which are sometimes difficult to define in the context of negotiations about objective demands and realities. The faculty, as the first party, may see its autonomy and self-respect at stake. Similarly, management may see its control slipping away. In the strictest sense of coming to a specific agreement, neither of these exoteric problems is germane. Yet they are like the weather that determines the possibilities of the day.

To pass from this initial stage of indiscriminate and maladaptive approaches to bargaining into a mature stage of development requires analysis and recognition of what collective bargaining is and what it is not. First, a more sophisticated awareness of bargaining as a limitative model seems essential if the community college is to maintain a values perspective as an institution of higher education rather than as an extension of the public school or a member of the industrial order. *As a model for organizational change, collective bargaining addresses group self-interests, not institutional reform.* This point is contested severely by teacher unions and deserves examination.

Second, collective bargaining is potentially a process for fostering collaboration and mutual understanding *if the model limitations are fully appreciated.* Bargaining brings many hazards to the health of the organization, but it also creates more social opportunities that can be exploited on behalf of the college and of the faculty welfare, which is never protected over the long term if the college suffers. Even in a small community college, the issues of governance are complex. Collective bargaining is an appropriate instrument for examining the faculty's self-interests with regard to material benefits and working conditions. When it is seen as a means of coping with the totality of issues facing the college, however, the seeds of betrayal are sown.

One of the first lessons learned in community college bargaining is how quickly external authority enters the arena if the bargaining model is not limitative and placed as a companion piece to other internal drives for organization development. The irrepressible distinction between organization development and contractual management is especially due, not to irremediable value-conflict between faculty and administration in either setting, but to collective bargaining legislation and its natural stimulation of external power. As these elements are applied in tandem to the existing socio-economic environment, forces are generated which grow beyond control of the faculty or the administration. In a contractual crisis, both the faculty and the administration may become caught in the middle and arrive at a point of asking, "How did we get into this situation?"

When bargaining is seen by either side as something more than a means of settling faculty working conditions, so that the details of governance and development must be spelled out, the negotiations are likely to become so exaggerated that they supersede the college's purposes. Good faith bargaining is essential to produce a fair agreement, but collective bargaining is not the college's *raison d'etre*. The faculty contract should serve as *one* of the documents of college governance, specifying salaries and related benefits, total working days and classroom contact hours, conditions of appointment, leave provisions, and grievance procedures (restricted to the terms of the contract and procedural arbitration). Such a contract sets definite limits on administrative authority and opens the opportunity for shared authority, but it does not determine the college structure and system of development. Putting the whole of a college into a single contract is like trying to catch sunbeams.

An orderly contract settlement usually is difficult under any conditions. Contract negotiations are not a periodic affair: they begin with organization and move to proposal preparations, the first stage of negotiations, mediation, impasse, and final crisis. These stages unfold at a tremendous cost of time and psychic energy. Then begins contract administration and a new round of preparations.

Though bargaining conflict is not unhealthy *prima facie*, protracted, constant contractual dispute does not contribute to the welfare of a college. A continual preoccupation with bargaining causes other elements of governance to bend to its service. Communication becomes much more difficult as suspicions about the "other side" mount. Emotions are too close to the surface, preventing a cool perception of significant forces, as opposed to vestigial ones, impacting the welfare of the college and the faculty. Issues are too easily distorted under the pressure to make gains or to prove administrative accountability in simplistic terms. Purely academic or intellectual concerns take second priority and even become subject to scorn.

The bleakness of this scenario is relieved only if there is mutual recognition that it does not have to be. Collective bargaining is a challenge to professionalism on both sides of the table. Is there a way of getting at the evolving quality of psychological group needs during negotiations without trying to frame these needs by specific contractual provisions? Can the process serve as a learning situation for both parties? If the drive to settlement becomes untracked by psychological or philosophical concerns, the model loses its definition again; but cannot mature attitudes be cultivated by a joint approach to identifying and separating those needs and concerns which demand attention in organization development? Memos of understanding or agreement to search for better cooperation through a dual track of governance may result. The dual-track approach may be aided by pre-negotiations workshops on bargaining simulation and appraisal.

Defining and controlling the scope of bargaining depends on a broader context of understanding where the college is headed and what bargaining means. It is on those issues which the parties agree cannot be handled effectively in bargaining that a joint approach outside of the bargaining process becomes possible. A joint commitment to a specific objective (for example, to develop a faculty rehabilitation program) is needed to keep the college goals in perspective. Later efforts, of course, should avoid goals displacement in order to maintain the commitment.[75]

It is easy to become cynical about bargaining and to assume that groups do not strive for growth. The discovery of potential growth patterns requires discriminatory powers on both sides that are mutually sustaining. If the management team approaches the bargaining table with the attitude that it must protect the college from invidious influences, it is not likely to perceive well the faculty's position. Conversely, if the faculty team comes with the attitude that it must save the college from tyrranical administration, it is not likely to learn much about the problems and constraints of administration. The latter usually are much greater in community college administration than faculty appear to know.

Any administration is capable of error. Those errors may have become enlarged in the faculty's mind. Similarly, faculty are capable of misperception and ignorance. Regressive arguments crop up if the spirit of inquiry and learning is not present. The administration may strive for regression. ("See how complex it is; let's go back.") The faculty may be unwilling to weigh the management information. ("If you don't stop hassling, we'll get a real union in here to knock heads.") The dynamics of the institution's life may not be clearly understood by either side. Despite this adversary relationship, a mutually held motivation to learn could turn the strong tangential effects of bargaining onto a path of growth. If there is an honest desire for shared authority and a commitment to elevating the issues apart from the contract, there may be hope for the model.

Some of the most astute observers of the impact of collective bargaining in community colleges believe that contracts can achieve a model of shared authority if sufficient faith in the model is present on both sides.[76] Where the concept has been missing too long, there are no doubt gains to be made in this direction through bargaining; but the danger in this course lies in local ineptitude and powerlessness in the face of the inexorable forces of centralization set into motion by non-restrictive negotiations.

Unionism and Centralization

Unfortunately, there is difficulty in achieving a well-defined model because of the ideological rhetoric infusing faculty unionism, which tends to confuse the bargaining role in governance. In its most militant form, faculty unionism is an expression of the general trade union movement. The proselytization carries the same sounds:

> Teachers unions offer a direct vehicle for radicalizing the workplace, and they also offer bridges to other workers.[77]

> Evidence that educational workers will fight on their own behalf is a prerequisite for creating enduring ties with militants in blue collar unions.[78]

> Now is the time to build solidarity — with those with whom we work and teach, and perhaps even more important, with those who perform the labor in this society.[79]

The perspective seems to be that the context for promoting and protecting higher education is class struggle. This brand of ideology among college faculty is curious. Given the uncertainty of work force mobility in the future, class lines may harden, but industrialization in the United States has not created strong class consciousness. It is difficult to imagine that this kind of appeal could convert large numbers of college faculty.

Even the more moderate advocacy, however, is a claim for faculty unionism as the best defense of the academy and the best vehicle for reform in education. There is no hint of the critique purpose of higher education through which institutional reform becomes possible. Rather, the advocacy is for a sinking into the industrial competitive system. As a means of advancing economic self-interests, this course of action is understandable; but as reform ideology, it fails to encompass the trends and value-shifts in a demoralized but restlessly yearning post-Vietnam/Watergate society.

Among the purposes of higher education, it is necessary to acknowledge that aim of illuminating the channels through which society is moving. Education raises questions about the materialistic tendencies and the violently competitive and destructive forces that threaten the public welfare. Classrooms speak of "community," of "cooperative order," of "land ethics," of "limits to growth." It becomes questionable whether a college faculty, plunging deep into a corporate style of behavior, can say anything meaningful about the greater needs of society.

Given the emerging power of the union, the problem is how to prevent a hardening of the arteries of college governance. It is clear what the big unions (for example, the American Federation of Teachers) have in mind: a consolidation of faculty interests which claims to be founded theoretically on a concept of community, but the vastness of which inhibits those values of community life associated with diversity, narrowing of social distance between disparate groups, and cohesion wrought primarily through informal, not the formal, organization. The following argument is revealing:

> [Unionization] provides an organized form of recognition of the fact that we are workers and that the most appropriate form of organization is in solidarity with other workers. From there the struggle begins to establish parity with management. Out of this struggle will come additional forms of organization for colleges and universities which move beyond defense of rights of workers to the effective control of all workplaces by those who do the work. Out of this struggle will come new relationships to the community and a new definition of the notion of community which has played such a significant role in the history of American philosophy.[80]

Several observers of higher education have commented on the evolvement of faculty unions toward greater political power through centralization and expansion of the membership base.[81] Just as labor unions have had great influence on public policy relevant to their concerns, a coalescence of faculty unions could bring great influence to bear on public education policy. It is precisely this expectation which is projected in faculty unionism.

It is the drive for political power that forms the root of centralization. A federal law for public sector collective bargaining would stimulate an even greater tendency in this direction.[82]

Though locked in struggle against each other, the two major unions (National Education Association and AFT) have called for consolidation,[83] but a "national union" need not evolve to complete the pattern of centralization. As unionization takes greater hold, a corresponding coalescence of higher education boards and agencies is likely to be triggered. (This pattern, of course, can be and is argued in reverse with the same result.) Centralized administration becomes even more necessary. Legislative action and judicial interpretation are increased as both power structures strive to influence public education policy. Power breeds counterpower. The legislative effect is described by Latham:

> The legislature referees the struggle, ratifies the victories of the successful coalitions, and records the terms of the surrenders, compromises, and conquests in the form of statutes . . . What may be called public policy is actually the equilibrium reached in the group struggle at any given moment, and it represents a balance which the contending factions constantly strive to weight in their favor . . . Defeated groups do not possess a veto on proposals and acts that affect them. But what they do possess is the right to make new combinations of strength . . . combinations that will support a new effort to rewrite the rules in their favor.[84]

It is not the accuracy of this scenario but the authenticity of its outline of a natural power progression that is chiefly contended here. The panorama of unfolding events also may be influenced by other community and human development trends. Furthermore, the concern is only partly with what may come to pass. More immediately, the point is to distinguish clearly between *political power* — the chief end of centralized authority — and *bargaining power*. This distinction is essential in order to define a model for collective bargaining appropriate to community college development apart from the tugs and pulls of unionization.

Obviously, faculties will be unionized as they pursue collective bargaining. The question remains as to how collective bargaining can be adapted without distorting academic and institutional development. Is this question being taken seriously? There are several dichotomies in the trend of unionization from which "yes" and "no" answers may be derived. For example, Ladd and Lipset show that election results throughout higher education do not agree with the percentages of expressed support for collective bargaining. In the case of community colleges, however, this observation is qualified by their finding that community college faculty are by far the strongest segment in favor of bargaining agents; therefore, they may be expected to follow through more decisively than their university counterparts when provided the opportunity to vote.[85] This greater decisiveness, however, does not necessarily mean that the issues are given less consideration.

There are conflicting positions among faculty groups in regard to the options available when enabling legislation is passed.[86] Usually this conflict is resolved in favor of affiliation with NEA or AFT, but some faculties have opted for independent units or smaller regional organizations without national affiliation (for example, in upstate New York, the Association of Community College Faculties.)[87] Other such organizations could emerge in the future. While the greater discrimination and even the survival of these independent organizations in the wake of larger forces remains to be seen, their existence is an encouraging sign of careful consideration of the stakes in unionization.[88]

It is through arrangements by which the identity of the college is best protected that the identity of the faculty as a professional group is best promoted. Independent faculty unions hold the most promise along these lines, which is not to say that the adversary relationship in local bargaining is necessarily less potent. The promise lies in a vision of controlled change that retains a dimension of institutional loyalty.

Allegiance and Bargaining

Many articles and studies suggest a number of causes for faculty unionism, some of which derive from local campus conditions, but there seems to be general agreement on three primary causes: (1) economic interests; (2) protection of job security; and (3) desire for greater participation in college governance. In community colleges, it seems fair to say that the first two issues are dominant.[89] Collective bargaining on these broad issues presumes that a public sector bargaining law exists which includes the community college in its coverage.[90] The nature of the law and arbitration by Public Employees Relations agencies provide some guidance in bargaining. However, in practice, the scope of bargaining generally is not constrained.[91] Community college enabling legislation also determines the context of bargaining since it provides for the college's sponsorship base and external authority relationships. Finally, civil service laws and retirement systems implemented prior to collective bargaining legislation may have implications for contract settlement and administration.[92]

Finding a critical path to a healthful contract settlement through this relatively uncharted labyrinth is an exercise that requires mature judgment and even statesmanship from both parties. Tactics are not enough. While winning tactics may bring singular victories, the long season requires both strategy[93] and analysis of environmental trends that minimize later entrapment in non-productive or stagnation-causal policies. The approach taken has a lot to do with where allegiance is placed.

The question of allegiance, however, is not one for faculty alone. The vital end commitment by all groups is not even to the college *per se*, but to the adaptive process by which it keeps moving as an institution. It always is difficult to know exactly what is going on. A management posture that measures loyalty to the organization only according to management's view of what the organization is and what it must become is more myopic than allegiant. By the same reasoning, perceived "irrationality" should not be of such concern as to cause the adoption of poorly initiated policies for the sake of removing it.[94] Each new contract automatically brings some tightening, which may or may not be sufficient for control under new conditions. The task of management is to *plan* change and *adapt* to it rather than merely to react to threatening forces.

For faculty as well, the future hinges on whether they will continue to give allegiance to the institution *as changing* or to the union, where the power obviously lies. It is a corporate power, however, that produces levelling effects. Leadership in the major unions is prone to remain fixed as it follows the greatest good for the greatest number. In consolidated unions, professional faculty could well become a minority in the future.

In bargaining, as distinct from unionism, there is another vehicle for demonstrating allegiance to greater ends than personal and political gains. Contrary to some elitist views heard from within higher education, there is considerable evidence that community college faculty have achieved professional identity which gives hope to this ideal of discrimination. For example, as far back as 1967, a national study of the attitudes of community college faculty discovered that they are "nearly unanimous in their desire that the junior college be genuinely considered a segment of higher education" and that there is deep concern about autonomy.[95] Bargaining may serve or destroy this sense of identity.

The value of allegiance does not stand isolated. It may be evoked or deepened by dialectical struggle. But a dialectical approach maximizes the use of ideology. It is better defined and sustained by continuing search and inquiry — a reasoning process that balances the drive to fulfill needs and wants with a greater search for understanding what it is that is being shaped as a result. In bargaining, where demands are made and served without care or insight into change to which both sides are actively and uncritically contributing, the path taken may lead to an undermining of faculty and institutional autonomy. Granted, the balance is difficult to achieve. The striving for it may bring the ultimate test of loyalty, as defined by Hirschman: "Loyalty is at its most functional when it looks most irrational, when loyalty means strong attachment because it is so much like another one that is also available."[96]

Of the three main issues cited as causes for unionization, most emphasis has been placed on economic gains in the first decade of collective bargaining. The emphasis may shift to job security, but the two are closely related. Unions remind us that, while men do not live by bread alone, they do live by bread; community college faculties have discovered that bargaining yields more "bread." In their empirical analysis of unions on campus, Baldridge and Kemmerer conclude that, on a national scale, faculty salaries have risen higher at colleges with bargaining agents than at those without agents.[97]

Angell adds, however, that these increases may have come at a cost of reduction of other services.[98] If so, it would be spurious to construe that the salary adjustments, therefore, were neither fair nor necessary; yet, in a steady-state budgeting situation, and especially in one that combines inflation with declining revenues, there must be limits to adjustment if a formula for effective institutional operation is to be maintained. It may be argued, in a particular bargaining case, that these limits have not been reached (a critical matter requiring resources analysis, which may be aided by cost-simulation models). The arguments then are vehemently pursued, particularly as "whipsaw" effects are felt. A test of allegiance in this case is made mutually, whether or not it is recognized, by the degree to which an honest and full exchange of information takes place.

Another counter-argument to the notion of limits is that the pie for education must be made bigger. Essentially, this argument merely broadens the analysis on a higher system level. More is at stake because such broadening introduces forecasting of institutional roles as well as cost analysis. Clearly, there are other public interests which are gaining parity in the competition for the tax dollar. Particularly in the light of a pending energy shortage, a continuing change of the work force and life-styles adds to the projection of a requirement of new resiliency. The protection of job security depends on this resiliency. Therefore, assessing the long-term interests of faculty, goes beyond building a greater power base. Power does not protect against institutional decline.

The resiliency stems from evaluation and development. It is perhaps in this connection that faculty desire for greater participation in governance ought to be tapped. A drama of irony develops when the issues of community college governance are separated, as they must be, from those issues facing the large universities and multi-campus systems which were experiencing greater statewide control prior to the advent of bargaining. The bureaucratic structures of the latter have tended to dissipate the faculty's authority, except perhaps in their disciplines. Community colleges, on the other hand, enjoy the advantage of relative smallness. Community college development still is graspable, at least in general terms, by the major groups which influence development. Even as a unit of a larger community college system with a central administration, the local campus may retain some autonomy. Whereas a shared-authority model may be *passé* in the multi-versity, it still has appropriateness for the community college. Failure to implement shared-authority concepts chiefly derives from insecurity, misunderstanding, and unwillingness to face complexity. The opportunity exists.

Again, however, concepts of shared authority should not become routinized through static policy provisions. While structure has a more definite cast, policies are continually subject to examination and change. Depending on the breadth and vitality of the issues involved, faculty may be instrumental in policy revision. There also are circumstances in which change may depend almost entirely on administrative initiative. (It is not difficult to see that the faculty as a whole is the most conservative group involved in governance.) In either case, *ad hocracy* may serve better than formal mechanisms.

In shared authority, it is difficult to enumerate specifically those items belonging to faculty and those belonging to administration. With the increase of specialized aspects of college governance, there is a need for continuing assessment by faculty of those areas where their influence can be most beneficial. One would expect academic affairs to be the center of attention (though such is not always the case). The number of faculty committees is not necessarily a sign of strength.

Indeed, a reduction in the number of standing committees in favor of academic task forces and *ad hoc* groups may contribute to greater faculty authority. To formalize such matters through contracted arrangements tends to reduce the vitality of the change process and sets up another debilitating side industry of grievance adjudication in which issues become "principles" that must be won regardless of the merits of the localized case. When this phenomenon begins to occur frequently, the shift of allegiance to the union is clearly visible.

Shared authority assumes, of course, that constitutional process exists, but a living constitution is not an anchor for vested interests and maintenance of the status quo. Rather, it is a sail which the institution uses to propel its orderly movement. The allegiance is always to the institution, not to power groups.

One of the surest signs of vitality in the constitutional process is the degree to which faculty and administration give voice to it. If the relationship between the two groups becomes overly adversary and delineated by highly specific provisions, the value of creative/critical voice is lessened. Governance is hardened. An example of this hardening of the lines may be seen in the general unionist posture on staff evaluation, which holds that evaluation is a supervisory responsibility. The disconnection from the traditional values assigned to participation in this task is clear. Another example is found in the typical view that staff development and rehabilitation are necessary to protect job security. While there is much value to the institution as well as to the faculty in protecting job security, it is not the primary value in staff development programs. Rather, staff development is the key to the maintenance of quality in carrying out educational missions. Increased job security is an important derivative benefit. By focusing on quality as a joint responsibility and concern, job security is strengthened in ways that do not accrue in a separatist model. Success and failure are shared.

The future of the community college is likely to bring serious problems of faculty tenure and threats of retrenchment. Only the most dynamic and creative efforts in evaluation and development, springing from interactive faculty and administrative leadership and a mutual desire for cooperation between groups, can provide the means for saving people in the organization. Contractual clauses calling for ritualistic attempts to find other positions for targeted faculty when financial exigency requires program cutbacks are likely to fail because they assign the task too late. The inevitable grievances undertaken by the union may compound a difficult situation; but if the potential areas of weakness have not been identified, and the faculty have lost their professional growth direction, the best that shall be said is that the situation was made difficult. This may be all that can be said in any case, but, in human affairs, there is much to be gained from a general will to grow.

In discussing allegiance and its place in the future of the community college, the middle-ground view is most open to criticism. There is something to be learned in this dialogue, too. If colleges do not persist with such values, by what measure do they remain collegial institutions? When these values disappear, the college may be a knowledge factory or a training institute, but it is not likely to have that climate which appeals to youth and to those older adults seeking renewal. If anomie is not radiant, allegiance, of course, does not disappear: human nature puts it somewhere in the scheme of transactions. The question is whether or not it can become a channelized transformational influence. The contention here is that, while allegiance can be fragmented, it cannot be equally distributed. Either the college or the union will be given primacy in the competing claims.

Bargaining, *per se*, is not a threat. Rather, it is in the accompanying formal organization that an integration of values is most difficult to achieve. In formal groups established for the legitimate pursuit of the members' self-interests, the members are turned inward to protectionist concerns. Evaluation and development programs are a secondary concern and are likely to be undertaken in a trivial manner if there is no direct connection to the main program for action: to obtain the goals of the organization. The argument even can be made that educational values are subject to trade if the group's immediate self-interests can be promoted as a result, and naturally so. In the political system, there is reliance on "countervailing power" (Galbraith) to prevent extreme damage.

The greater problem of educational reform requires some intellectual commitment and spirit of independence from doctrine: these qualities are not enhanced by preoccupation with the group's self-interests alone. To some extent, community colleges always have struggled with this problem; contract settlement and administration merely heightens it. While it remains difficult to sort out the conflicting standards and values, community college educators already have proven by their achievement of the past 25 years that they are not those men described by Aeschylus who, "like the shapes of dreams, handle all things in bewilderment and confusion." By recognizing the inherent conflict, hope is raised for a resolution that serves to the best extent possible the long-term interests of the college as well as the self-interests of the faculty. In such a resolution, there is achieved from the adversarial nature of bargaining an earned victory.

Future Issues and "Oughts"

An important point made by Leslie is that one of the institutional factors affecting collective bargaining is "the level of conflict experienced over time."[99] Where the relationship between faculty and administration has been seriously affected by unhealthy conflict for some time, a negotiated settlement may come as a blessing to both sides, even if it is heavy in its specific provisions of governance. The subjective theme of this analysis is that there is no formula for uniform settlement in collective bargaining. Needs and circumstances differ from campus to campus. It is only as we allow the ambience of trends and events to color the perception of local conditions as a reflection of the projected general condition that a model of uniformity takes hold. The major premise is that shared – authority concepts are still possible with collective bargaining, but that the relative state of the college environment will set the more definitive possibilities and requirements.

With some misgiving, therefore, this concluding section generalizes further on some primary issues which are so applicable to bargaining and administration that they are likely to be universally experienced, however successful or unsuccessful the excursion into faculty contracts has been. These issues are: unit determination, grievance adjudication, tenure and re-appointment, and the right to strike.

The selection of these issues as the primary ones is based on a review of the literature on collective bargaining in higher education, which, fortunately, is beginning to grow rapidly.[100] While there is general agreement about the centrality of these issues, positions taken on each are less generally shared. This again illustrates the uncertainty in this field, which, in one sense, is a healthy sign of opportunities yet unrealized and, in another, a further reminder of the need for caution and critical reflection. While Keatsian wisdom would tell us that we should neither dispute nor assert, but "whisper results to our neighbor," collective bargaining is not a whispering affair. The emphasis here is on community college development in the light of these issues.

The pioneering colleges perhaps did not realize fully the major importance of unit determination. Once the unit is determined, it is difficult to change that determination. While the legislation and arbitration in regard to unit determination usually does not create a clear pattern, for the most part, it lends to a very broad interpretation of what staff positions may be included in the unit. NLRB arbitration of industrial cases gives disciplinary authority to the union over its members, including those members with supervisory responsibilities.[101] As Baldridge and Kemerer point out, PERBS tend to introduce practices based on industrial experience.[102] Such authority, combined with the precariousness of a supervisory member's status in a bargaining situation, makes it essential that middle-level administrators, especially, have protection and guidance in their roles. It is they who must work directly with the faculty.

It is in the college's best interests (and perhaps in the interest of the administrator's integrity), however, that administrative staff not be part of the faculty bargaining unit. If they are included in the unit, the problem is even more difficult. But, in either case, the future is likely to make life in the middle exceptionally unsettled if administrative status and roles vis-a-vis bargaining units are not clear. If middle administration loses its confidence, the college development will suffer. Additionally, the question will occur as to why a well-qualified staff member should assume administrative responsibilities under such circumstances. If the person enjoys tenured academic rank, the temptation is strong to return to the more certain status of full-time teaching. Another recourse for the administrative staff is to seek to establish its own bargaining agent; but, again, the issue of unit determination is raised immediately.

College trustees and other higher authorities should consider the problem of administrative support and morale as a crucial agenda item in the next few years. Hopefully, a new qualitative dispatch in the arbitration of higher education issues also will begin to occur. With arbitration, the focus shifts to grievance adjudication — an area even more replete with potential for disequilibrium.

Arbitrators do not always understand that administration is an art as well as a science of procedures. Contracted procedures must be followed. In substantive matters, however, judgment obtains that is not always reducible to a statement of scientific merit. For pessimists (or informed optimists), there is much evidence in the history of grievances for the view that collegiality is gone forever and that, henceforth, governance will be mechanistically formal. Those who wish to preserve or to begin a shared-authority model should recognize that this hope is pinned to a grievance system which envelops the specific provisions of the contract only and which is limited to procedural arbitration.

"Past practices" clauses ought to be stoutly resisted on behalf of organization development. It also may be argued that such clauses do not contribute to faculty self-interests in the long term. Grievances over departure from past practice, particularly when they are trivial or frivolous, represent a strong thrust toward rigidity. Change is a factor of institutional survival; its orderly occurrence should not be unduly restricted. On the other hand, the governance structure ought to provide for faculty participation in the change process. Arbitrarily forced change may result in past practice proposals. It is difficult to find a proper balance in these matters, but, again, collaboration in evaluation and development is the best guarantee against arbitrary or capricious change. By law, judicial interpretation, and contracted grievance procedures, the faculty's individual rights are well protected. A "past practices" clause is not likely to protect them more, but so far as organization health is concerned, it has a divergent, negative connotation.

An equal or greater danger to autonomous functioning is contained in substantive arbitration. Unions tend to press for arbitral review in nearly all matters of administration. Relief from this pressure is possible only if the faculty leadership maintains a policy of scrutinizing the merits of each grievance before agreeing to assume it as a group interest. Since this quality control is undependable, the control also needs to be implemented by an arbitration provision which clearly limits outside authority. This limitation may be mutually beneficial to the college and the faculty on many issues. The die seems to be cast, however, for arbitral review in tenure and non-reappointment cases, which becomes substantive because of the singular impact of the actions.

Garbarino and Aussieker maintain that "the strongest force working for faculty unionism in the future is the continuing vigorous attack on job security and tenure."[103] Unions may be expected to push strongly for arbitral review in non-reappointment or dismissal matters. For several reasons, community colleges ought to prepare for substantive arbitration in nearly all dismissal cases. It is coming because of the tradition of substantive review in tenured faculty cases and because of the nature of arbitration. The concept of tenure itself may give way to the industrial variety of job security. Is tenure necessary as a protection where faculty members also are protected by a contract?[104]

The original principle of tenure as a guarantee of academic freedom has lost much of its strength in the community college, if tenure ever was won on that ground. Tenure is, quite simply, job security. It is rendered and received as job security, usually without respect to departmental quotas, which are more in vogue in the universities. In discussing job security, the emphasis is placed more correctly on loyalty and ethics than on freedom. An individual who has given many years of service to the institution surely is entitled to loyalty from the institution. To dismiss this value says something about the morality of the organization. At the same time, this loyalty should not be so unqualified that security turns into stagnancy. The tenured faculty member owes loyalty, too, which is best expressed through his or her "staying alive" in the true educational sense. Facing a steady state, if not a state of declining enrollments, community colleges may experience this professional growth problem increasingly as faculty turnover slows significantly. Where is the loyalty and justice, or the common sense, in protecting tenured faculty in programs which have remained static while sacrificing untenured faculty in more dynamic programs? Obviously, programs and faculty evaluation are key factors in balancing the institutional needs and obligations.

It is possible that, within the next five years, most community college faculty could enjoy tenure with many years of service ahead before retirement. In 1974, tenure percentages were reported to be at the 70 to 75 per-cent level.[105] The doors will not be open for many new teaching professionals in the 1980s. The prospect of an elite group is strange in an institution which is created essentially as a fulfillment of democratic concepts in higher education; its existence should bring increasing pressure for accountability from disaffected graduates longing for a teaching career as well as from outside groups and agencies. This pressure is perhaps the main reason why unionism is seen as the best defense of faculty job security. Under these circumstances, however, tenure would have no special meaning since nearly every faculty member would have it.

The major implication of this levelling force against tenure, inadvertently promoted by unionism and "the future as history" (Heilbroner), is not in its threat to job security, in the name of which it operates, but that it also removes the justification for permanent rank. Not all community colleges have academic rank systems, but those that do will experience the closing of this sub-system as the higher ranks are used up. Indeed, it is a closing of the extrinsic rewards system as a whole that necessitates a new emphasis on intrinsic rewards through evaluation dialogue referencing change factors. Everyone could become a "full professor", but not without economic levelling. Rank systems could be negotiated out as substantive arbital review is negotiated in . If the rank system is to remain with any validity, it will need the flexibility of demotion as well as promotion. In a closed system, the only mobility possible is one which is downward as well as upward. Such a system ought to retain peer review and administrative review as a balanced approach to handling the inevitable conflict.

Job security and related job status are value issues which impact the college's development. It seems certain that job security will be the number-one issue on the bargaining table. This issue embraces a number of other considerations, such as program retrenchment and FTE ratios. It may become the chief motivator of strike action.

The right to strike ought to be granted. Anti-strike provisions are a crucial question in regard to the law. Where the strike is illegal, as it is in most states with public sector bargaining laws, it often is argued in bargaining that, since the right to strike must be given up, *quid pro quo* is in order. Arbitration clauses have been won, for example, on this basis. Yet, in a serious impasse, the strike weapon is seldom removed from the strategy. Baldridge and Kemerer report that 80 per cent of the union chairpersons they surveyed agreed that the strike is a legitimate weapon.[106] The authors seem quite correct in their conclusion that faculty will strike if they feel it is necessary. Strikes have occurred, of course, in spite of harsh penalties to faculty.[107] It is not only this reality, however, that suggests a revision.

The prospect of a college campus locked by a strike has long been an anathema to the professional conscience, and there is no question that it represents serious disequilibrium. The aftermath of a strike may be bitter, but far worse is the emasculation of professional interests and responsibilities that occurs in a deliberate "slow down" just short of a strike. When professionals work, their commitment should not be qualified. Indeed, qualification tends to destroy professional commitment. A strike usually is not undertaken lightly by faculty. It is possible that the issues separating the two parties can be resolved only by a strike, but in such case, the issues are really nailed down. While doing everything possible to prevent it, the administration should learn to accept a strike with less trepidation than the threat usually evokes. It is a hard lesson to learn but perhaps necessary for the future. A strike does affect the welfare of students, of course, a point that must be well considered by the faculty who feel driven to it; yet the withdrawal of teaching services does not pose as much danger to the public welfare as, for example, the withdrawal of police protection. Greater danger to the profession of education is engendered by illegal or unethical actions. The right to strike permits closure in the bargaining process without these hazardous actions.

The welfare of students is affected by the outcomes in all of these areas. For this reason, a fifth main issue of the future might be the place of students at the bargaining table. The universality of this issue would seem to depend on how well community colleges survive the impact of collective bargaining. Particularly as older clienteles are attracted to the community college, the sophistication of students with regard to the bargaining issues and their stake in the outcomes is likely to rise. Unions argue that faculty interests are in accord with student interests. When raised, this proposition also should be tested at the bargaining table by weighing the effects of the various proposals and counterproposals on a scale of student welfare.

Finally, ''collective bargaining impact'' conferences, dealing exclusively with the community college sector, should be convened by those organizations which have the needed resources to bring together faculty leaders, administrators, student government officers, trustees, and legislators for constructive dialogue on the future of ''community'' and those associated values which have so far distinguished this institution.

The worst possible impact of collective bargaining would be a diminution of the commitment to these values, which are expressed outwardly in the general education functions of the college. The challenge of general education reform is far more inspiring to the leadership qualities of faculty and administration alike. It is to this topic that we turn next.

Summary

Collective bargaining, in its first decade on the community college campus, has been fraught with turmoil and uncertainty. Bargaining is here to stay, but there is a need to grasp the process more firmly and to come to a better accommodation through more precise understanding of the inherent values conflict. Collective bargaining is seen as a potential growth pattern if it is fostered as a limitative model. Bargaining is compatible with shared-authority concepts if bargaining power is dis-

VALUES AND THE FUTURE

tinguished from political power. The latter is the chief end of centralization. There are hazards in the bargaining process which can turn it onto
a path of betrayal for the college and faculty if the stimulation of
external authority is not calculated. The allegiance of faculty and
administration to the institution as changing is a prime factor in the
maintenance of autonomy and a sense of identity. Collective bargaining forces attention on resources allocation, which can be positive; but
if this attention is too exclusive, the constant revitalization of higher
education purposes becomes undermined. Unions exist to promote the
self-interests of faculty. College evaluation and development are better
fostered through a cooperative rather than an adversarial approach.
The adversary relationship in bargaining need not result in disequilibrium, but there are serious issues that are likely to be universally
experienced in the future of the community college. These are unit
determination, grievance adjudication, tenure and non-reappointment,
and the right to strike. Attention is turned to general education.

TOWARD A NEW HOUSE OF GENERAL EDUCATION

At a Boston "town meeting" held during America's bicentennial year, Henry Steele Commager was gravely pessimistic about the world's future. As he spoke of the problems of population growth, uncontrolled exploitation of natural resources, environmental damage beyond recovery, and the increasing probability of nuclear warfare, the nation's dean of historians was echoing a prophecy of grave danger to human survival that has been articulated by many of the world's most astute observers with increasing urgency during the past 15 years. A similar pessimism is felt in all of our institutions struggling, but not quite succeeding, to revitalize their missions for coping with unprecedented, dynamically complex problems. In Commager's view and in the views of those who contribute to a similar analysis, mankind is at a turning point.

This pessimism is not universally shared. But the observation that man has reached a criticial turning point seems to be crystallized in current thinking about man and society, whatever the individual reflections may be about hope for the future. This observation is stimulated by the knowledge that science is broadening its scope and deepening its power. Biological science, for example, is on the verge of creating life itself.

What is presented here is not a theoretical overview, but a series of propositions and arguments about general education and an attempt to defend their validity. This is done by referencing the changing role and relationships of the contemporary sciences and incorporating as pragmatically as possible those values of general education which, fortunately, still are the subject of much discussion.

A New World View

Today, a new world view is emerging. Education may not yet have caught up with it, but it already is influencing the directions of many different professions and fields of study. Unlike other "Copernican revolutions," it has many leaders and spokesmen who, though contributing to the general store of knowledge in different ways, are more aware of the connections between fields and their participation in creating a new *Weltanschauung*. Maslow, for example, clearly expressed this awareness when he called the change "a spirit of the age." Humanistic psychology, in its development of a new image of man, was seen by Maslow to be "paralleled by independent advances and discoveries in other fields as well."[108] Laszlo captured the spirit of the new world view in these thoughts directed at the general reader:

> The contemporary sciences are in a period of rapid growth and transformation . . . If there is continuity in science, that is, if we can discern an enduring trend, we can already say something not only about the kind of world picture which is in process of taking shape today, but also about the contours of the concept which we will find increasingly defined and specified in the near future . . . A new world view is taking shape in the minds of advanced scientific thinkers the world over, and this view is our best hope of understanding and controlling the processes that affect the lives of us all.[109]

Laszlo is a general systems philosopher. General systems theory illustrates a methodological dimension of the new world view in the same way as does the structural analysis of contemporary anthropology. It is a moving away from the reductionist approach of highly specialized investigation to a position of *holistic thinking*. There are multivariate origins of the holistic systems approach, but the shift from reductionism to holism, or at least an acknowledgement of the necessity of complementary approaches, is found especially in biological science. Ludwig von Bertalanffy, considered to be one of the fathers of general systems theory, was at first a systems biologist. In the field of medicine, a parallel development of theory emerged in the late 1930s with Kurt Goldstein, who had great influence on Maslow.

In Goldstein's biological theory, the fundamental principle is that each organism always must be studied as a whole. By this, he meant the individual whole, interacting with its environment, but "still the individual . . . not a community of individuals."[110] As Grene explains:

> He is recommending as primary to biology, attention to the living individual rather than to its parts in isolation: analogously to the insistence of some biochemists that experiments should be conducted as far as possible *in vivo*

> rather *in vitro*. In the study of organisms, he is insisting,
> whatever is partial is distorted, if not artificial . . . Yet, he
> insists, one must deal clinically and experimentally with the
> specifiable particulars of the whole . . . He is never suggest-
> ing the abandonment of precise methods, which *can* only
> handle parts, but only the constant reference through these
> to the nature of the whole.[111]

There are many more implications in the clinical use of this principle, but Goldstein is cited merely to indicate a change in the use of the empirical method necessitated by a change in the entire focus of investigation, from parts to wholes. Several other early examples also could be used. The point is that, as this shift began to occur in several fields, a new view of the world was in the making.

The Goldstein example gives rise to a second point, which is that, as a holistic approach takes hold, the connections between the disciplines become more clear, and the tendency for interdisciplinary borrowing to effect new general fields of study becomes more pronounced. The advent of socio-biology or bio-ethics are cases in point. The field of Organization Development, discussed in the preceding chapters, is a further verification of this trend. Bennis, for example, did not hesitate in using a metaphor of the healthy personality to arrive at his criteria of organization health. Moreover, what seems to be occurring is a gradual narrowing of the gap between science and philosophy. Indeed, it may be that less significance should be placed on the interdisciplinary trend of the last decade than on the strengthening of bonds between science and philosophy. Kuhn's analysis of scientific paradigms and the way in which scientific revolutions occur, first published in 1962, is one of those contributions which enable science to be seen more clearly in a social context.[112]

The result is that science no longer can be seen as value-free. It is not simply a matter of understanding that science is more than a piecemeal accumulation of facts or that the questions chosen for scientific investigation reflect valuation. These attributes now are more commonly accepted, but the relations of science and the public interest, which now are being dramatically worked out, also portend a change in the world view. Even scientists are not so certain about the unimpeded nature of scientific progress or that scientific questions should be left to the scientific community. Who decides on the questions which are clearly ethical in nature, for example, those questions in genetics research?[113]

Part of this uncertainty is due to the recognition that science was shaped in an historic context which gave it a normative structure. As modern science emerged in the 16th Century when major institutional changes were underway, its survival under the pressures of church and state took the course of focusing on rationality, empiricism, and materialist reality, separating out the normative, a-rational, and subjective approaches to phenomena. In doing so, it separated mind from matter. The scientific view which emerged was a positivistic determination that nature could be changed and, indeed, science has proved it to be so. As Francis Bacon saw, scientific knowledge is power. But now it is also seen that science crosses nature like a road. The scientist is becoming more aware of the implications of that crossing: nature's inhabitants do not know about roads, and there is much beyond that is not seen. It is this awareness that is pushing science closer to philosophical reflection.

It is interesting that science, which has penetrated the universities so thoroughly since the mid-19th Century, was an outsider until that time. Science did not enter education through the traditional schools, but through new institutions. When science finally entered the university, it stepped back from society in the name of its objectivity, yet it had shown its capacity to stimulate and direct technological development. Science reinforced and was reinforced by the industrial revolution. Though the distinctions between science and technology remain clear, the ramifications of these relationships now are equally clear. Science is not losing but gaining power; however, in its new world view, the claim of objectivity is questioned. Especially in the social sciences, the current questioning is very strong. There is a real weakness in an epistemology which separates subjectivity and non-empirical data in fields in which these elements cannot be ignored.

Science may be the best way of knowing, but it is not the only way of knowing. On the fringes of science have always been those fields of interest which, though excluded because they did not fit into the rationalist, empirical mode, would not go away. These are the para-sciences and, as they are termed in some quarters, the "pseudo-sciences". It is difficult to find an appropriate designation, for there is a great variety of activity in these fields, and a good deal of charlatanism has accompanied the popularization of them. If there is one violation that science cannot abide, it is fraud. However, after making some distinctions between "para" and "pseudo", it will be seen that, in the field of parapsychological study there is a body of knowledge and an impressive literature that places the phenomena of extra-sensory perception and psychokinesis well beyond dismissal. Though unenthusiastically, science now accepts parapsychology as a legitimate study; but the long hesitation to do so is instructive about science. With a few exceptions, including the important exception of the Rhine laboratory at Duke University, universities under the control of science have not contributed much to the accumulation of parapsychological knowledge. Like science prior to the 19th Century, the parasciences have had to go around the university.[114]

Paranormal data are still regarded as more of an embarrassment than anything else by empirical schools, and understandably so, for the existence of the psi process shakes their foundation. How is it possible that the mind can make contact with matter directly without the evidence of the senses? As Louisa Rhine concluded, "The idea that the only avenue to the mind lies through the senses is outmoded."[115] The broadening of science by the inclusion of parapsychology has not reduced the importance of empirical methodology, but it forces the social sciences — following well behind the physical sciences — to recognize that the world experienced through the senses is not the total reality and may be illusionary. In summing up the case for parapsychology, Koestler concludes:

> It is time for us to draw the lessons from twentieth-century post-mechanistic science, and to get out of the strait-jacket which nineteenth-century materialism imposed on our philosophical outlook. Paradoxically, had that outlook kept abreast with modern science itself, instead of lagging a century behind it, we would have been liberated from that strait-jacket long ago . . . We have become a good deal cleverer since [sixteenth century], but not much wiser in knowing what it all means. But once this is recognized, we might become more receptive to phenomena around us which a one-sided emphasis on physical science has made us ignore; might feel the draught that is blowing through the chinks of the causal edifice; pay more attention to confluential events; include the paranormal phenomena in our concept of normality . . .
>
> The consequences of such a shift of awareness are unforeseeable, and one cannot help but sympathize with the considered statement by Professor H.H. Price that "psychical research is one of the most important branches of investigation which the human mind has undertaken,"

that it seems likely "to throw entirely new light upon the nature of human personality and its position in the universe"; and that in time "it may transform the whole intellectual outlook upon which our present civilization is based".[116]

Finally, there is in this new world view a concern about man's future. The future always has been a concern, of course, but there is a difference in conception. The concern is active, not passive, based on a realization that problems of the present are not made in the present and are not resoluble in the present. The present, therefore, must be viewed from a perspective of the future as well as of the past. Futurism — models and theories about the future — is a formal study not universally accepted by those who have contributed to a dynamic sense of the future in the present, but there is a recognition in much of the literature on the social role of the contemporary sciences that "a new transformation is occurring in the circumstances of human life — new in the history of man and of the planet."[117] The recognition extends to man's participation in a dynamically unfolding but unifying process in nature. The power of science is deepened because it is now concentrating on both the differentiation and the integration of nature, a duality which must be as balanced as nature seeks a balance. (The concept is similar, perhaps, to that of individuality within community, discussed in Chapter Four.) It is a rediscovery of the oneness in all things and a consequent improved understanding of the necessity to calculate anew the power and the limitations of science.

Each age has explained the world according to its dominant knowledge and prevailing systems of belief. The change of world views does not necessarily replace "wrong" theories with "right" ones.[118] Rather, it is a shift of vision, a new way of seeing even the same phenomenon, as partly explained in this statement by Kuhn:

> Since remote antiquity most people have seen one or another heavy body swinging back and forth on a string or chain until it finally comes to rest. To the Aristotelians, who believed that a heavy body is moved by its own nature from a higher position to a state of natural rest at a lower one, the swinging body was simply falling with difficulty. Constrained by the chain, it could achieve rest at its low point only after a torturous motion and a considerable time. Galileo, on the other hand, looking at the swinging body, saw a pendulum, a body that almost succeeded in repeating the same motion over and over again *ad infinitum*. And

having seen that much, Galileo observed other properties of the pendulum as well and constructed many of the most significant and original parts of his new dynamics around them. From the properties of the pendulum, for example, Galileo derived his only full and sound arguments for the independence of weight and rate of fall, as well as for the relationship between vertical height and terminal velocity of motions down inclined planes. All these natural phenomena he saw differently from the way they had been seen before.[119]

This brief overview suggests that the way the world looks to science today is different than it looked in the last generation. Because of the need to accommodate new knowledge and beliefs, the scientific paradigm or "conceptual scheme" (Conant) changes. Sometimes, the change is merely an expansion, as, for example, the change in the social sciences from early positivism to the analytic framework of the disciplines in the 20th Century. But a change in science, however significant, does not in itself result in a new view of the world.

As many fields and professions begin to alter their vision, a major shift occurs. It is suggested that the characteristics of this shift are: (1) a trend toward holistic thinking and approaches; (2) a reassessment of the values in science; (3) a narrowing of the gap between philosophy and science, resulting in new images of man and nature; (4) a broadening of the scope of science; and (5) a recognition that man is on a new threshold of development in which the power of science must be calculated and turned more certainly to his favor.

There are, of course, several consequences for general education, assuming that education should contribute to a vision of the world that is at or near the actual existing state of knowledge. These consequences also are matters of interpretation in which arguments and assumptions rise and fall. The following sections explore these kinds of considerations.

Why General Education

Students come to and go through college in a great mix of experiential patterns. For some, it is a fleeting experience which leaves no mark: they come and go like people taking a short cut through campus on their way to someplace else. For others, college is a social blossoming: they get involved in activities, become student aides, seek out faculty members as friends, use the gym. These are the students who prove that the college can be a community. Toward the end of reducing the size of the first group and building the latter, there can be little question about the essential role of counselors, student advisors, and paraprofessional aides responsible for co-curricular and recreational programs. These programs represent another avenue for personal growth and achievement, one which sometimes is more enriching than the curriculum itself.

Whatever the experience, however, the nucleus is always the program — whether career or liberal arts — in which the student is enrolled. However good or poor the instruction, whether or not it holds the student's interest — the curriculum of instruction is the primary material out of which an educational experience is formed. The curriculum objectives, clear or unclear in the student's mind, represent the hope of his or her becoming a better educated, skilled individual more able to participate in a changing society and work environment.

Community college students always have been vocationally oriented. College is a path to an occupation or career. For this reason, occupational programs have been much emphasized in recent years. In the late 1960s, the call went out for "career education."[120] The distinction between career education and general education, however, is fallacious, and the fallacy grows more dangerous as higher education enrollments remain high while the intersection of educational and training programs with the actual job markets and career opportunities deteriorates. The revolution of rising expectations which has prevailed throughout this century, fed by the egalitarian force of education, is being countered today by work-force realities in the present industrial organization of society. Current underemployment trends are likely to remain strong, according to the most recent analyses of the work force, for at least the next decade.[121] While the speculative nature of these forecasts should be recognized, such developments offer compelling reasons for a shift away from specialized occupational programs toward a renewal of general education. The reasons are practical as well as philosophical.

There is no evidence that the increasing specialization of work force needs will not continue. However one may shudder at the prospect of the mega-machine, technological development is not diminishing. Technological change means that applied knowledge has a short life. Examples abound of worker transcience and job obsolesence in the work environment. Occupational shifting is a major characteristic of industrial society.[122] Nor is there, today at least, any reliable means through technological forecasting or manpower projections for determining specifically what jobs will be available in the future.

Is it the task of publicly-supported educational institutions to train specialists for industrial markets when it is known that most specializations have an obolescent nature? Is it not their task instead to give students a vocational perspective in a broad area of work through education in basic concepts and skills which may lead to an easier grasp of specific skills required on the job — and which may further lead them to the understanding that education is a lifelong process? Is it not also their task to transcreate this perspective in such a way that students become aware of the underlying forces and value-conflicts which impact their future? The social role of public higher education, at the undergraduate level at least, is more important than its role of service to industrial organization, for it is in the fulfillment of the social role that society benefits.

This should not be construed as a plea to "save the liberal arts." The community college movement hastened the demise of the "liberal arts tradition" as an elitist concept in higher education several years ago.[123] Continued attempts to dichotomize the meanings of "liberal arts" and general education, at least in the community colleges, are more misleading than the dichotomies of general and career education. Moreover, the broad vocational areas — such as allied health and the business and engineering technologies — fit well as missions of a community college. As a result of the depressed marketability of a baccaulearate degree, students today are seeking these programs in greater numbers. This shift demonstrates clearly that a college education is expected to lead to a good job. But if the same cycles of oversupply and obsolescence continue as in the past, a sense of betrayal may permeate all of education. Education must begin to register another, better reason for learning.

If general education is to contribute to a biophilus system of values that permits a transcendence of the purely technological forces shaping society, there first is a need for a revitalization of the traditional aims of education.

Some Educational Propositions

Assuming that the institutional purpose of the comprehensive community college is clear, the most fundamental questions facing its faculty are: (1) What should be taught? (2) How do we keep abreast of changing methodologies and conceptions in our academic fields?

In the development of the college's educational missions, attention naturally turns to the questions of instructional methodology: How can teaching techniques be varied so as to capture the interest of students with different learning rates and styles? What about team-teaching? How can closed-circuit television be used effectively? Individualized learning units? What should be done for students with emotional problems or physical handicaps? How can learning be measured? Questions of this type are most prevalent in current discourse on education, and they are, of course, important. Even to acknowledge the importance of teaching methods and strategies in this way is like a reminder of Holmes' "To a Catydid": "Thou sayest an undisputed thing in such a solemn way!"

The first proposition to be offered here about general education reform is that *these questions are secondary to the cognitive questions of how knowledge is conceptualized*. In some education schools, this proposition is reactionary and therefore demands explanation. Before moving into educational philosophy, however, there are a series of complementary propositions, all of which should be tied together. They are:

1. The specialized nature of the academic disciplines, along with discipline language barriers, represents a major obstacle to the creation of a unified structure of general education at the community college level.

2. There is a need to make much better use of general philosophy, which is trans-disciplinary and values-oriented, in general education.

3. All education is a preparation for the future.

4. Futuric concerns are expressed in all disciplines.

5. The evocation of perspectives of the future can and should be included as an objective in general education programs.

6. Neither general education, professional education, nor futures study are disciplines; all require a holistic approach.

To establish a clearer framework for argumentation, the emphasis here on curriculum content sets aside such tangential elements as grading practices, advisement, and class size. These are teaching strategy concerns. It is assumed, however, that the teaching will involve a heterogeneous student population consisting, for example, of educationally disadvantaged students who need remedial instruction or whose sub-culture gives them a somewhat different perspective than that of the college majority. These students may need special programs to assist them in their adjustment to the college environment as well as counselors who will follow their progress. For this reason, counselors should be directly involved in curriculum development, perhaps through assignment to particular academic divisions. Any special programs which include specific courses, however, should not construe these courses to be separate entities for meeting personal needs through a "watering down" of the subject matter. Not all courses have cognitive objectives, of course, but if the affective aims require the introduction of a principle or theory also used in another course, it is a disservice to oversimplify intentionally. The complexity of truth stands unbridled. Part of the challenge of community college teaching is to bring students to an understanding of that complexity. In the main, they are capable of grasping it through good teaching.

This caveat is offered not merely as a concern for quality, but even more as an assumption that, if general education is to contribute to the identification of a new system of human values and relationships more appropriate to the changing circumstances of society, the structure of general education, while flexible, must be consistently sound.

Finally, perhaps there should be some refinement of the key question, "*What* should be taught?" In accordance with the comments in the preceding section on the evanescent nature of specialized knowledge application, the "*what*" does not necessarily refer to subject matter but to concepts and approaches by which information takes on meaning. In other words, the "what" is actually a *how* — not "how to teach" but "how to learn."

It is on this point that confusion sometimes arises when general education faculty, including most community college faculty, are reminded of the need to keep abreast of knowledge in their fields. As generalists, who, for the most part, are concerned with broad fields of knowledge (for example, the field of sociology rather than a specialized research area in sociology), obviously they will not always have the most recent information available in the field. Authoritative data are indispensable, of course, but this is no reason to go on information crusades. Even the quantitative approach is interesting primarily as a methodology. Rather, the attention is better directed at new, major developments and concepts. Generalizations are sought which require, of course, explanation and documentation and are subject to criticism.

General scholarship of this kind is equally as demanding as the research which leads to new knowledge; it also requires creativity and devotion and is fraught with just as much uncertainty and risk. General education, after all, is a dynamic vocation. Those who enter general education as teachers must approach it as such. In almost every field, from astronomy to secretarial science, the instructor who learned principles and concepts 10 years ago but has made no effort to continue conceptual inquiry and relational work cannot really contribute in a vitalic way to general education. He may contribute in other ways to the college community, but his field has moved beyond his competence. *On this basis alone*, of the necessity for every instructor to maintain his professional competence, all the privileges not granted in the business and industrial occupations — extended summer vacations, recesses, sabbatical leaves, and so forth — are justified. They are not rewards but the means of professional renewal.

Some Philosophical Arguments

In *The Reforming of General Education* (which should be required reading in professional education), Bell concludes:

> The nature of college education can now be envisaged as a series of logical steps in which first comes the acquisition of a general background, second the training in a discipline, third the application of this discipline to a number of relevant subjects, and forth the effort to link the disciplines in dealing with common problems. It is this progression, involving at each step of the way an awareness of conceptual innovation and method, that is the heart of ordering a curriculum.[124]

This model effectively lays out the pattern for developing faculty commitment to general education. In effect, they are struggling with the third and fourth steps. It is not a satisfactory model for general education in the community college, however, because of the two-year curriculum limitations. Usually, the organization of general education does not get beyond the introduction of the disciplines, or if it does, there is apt to be a loss of conceptual frameworks by which knowledge is seen to be in a fluid state.

A student's file of notes depicts fairly well the way he is introduced to knowledge structure. If he is a secretarial science student, for example, the file on core subjects may run together because the connections are easily made; but he is careful to keep sociology separate from economics and literature. To allow them to become mixed would be disastrous to an orderly study approach. The fact that there are connections between these and other disciplines in a truer conceptualization is not a part of the learning model. This picture may be somewhat over-drawn, but an accurate description of general education could not state very much about the connective tissues of the system. They are in sad shape even though the individual courses may be quite healthy. For this reason, "liberal arts", especially, has lost much of its force as a program.

The disciplinary system was a good one for producing poten-tial English majors, psych majors, chemistry majors, and so forth, in those days when the transfer function of the community college was an avid concern ("will it transfer?"). Students did transfer with aca-demic success, the main criterion of outcomes analysis. The criterion always was suspect, of course, and conditions today have moved so far beyond transfer concerns that it no longer can be taken seriously. The disciplines will remain — indeed, they are vital — but there is no longer much doubt that an integration must be achieved. The system needs revitalization.

Does educational philosophy assist in this task of revitalizing general education? If it is not seen as a separate branch of philosophy, cut off from the mainstream of general philosophy, it may well contribute to a revitalization. Fortunately, there is evidence of a *rapprochment* bet-ween general philosophy and educational philosophy which holds promise of a better understanding of the relationships between theory and practice and a deeper knowledge of the place of general education.

The term "revitalization" is used because what seems most warranted is to look first at the traditional aims of general education. For example, it is through general education that a person develops his abilities to think effectively in both the logical and imaginative senses of the term, to communicate effectively (that is, to express himself clearly in speech and writing so as to be understood by others), to understand the meaning of competence in a field of endeavor, to clarify and discriminate among val-ues and value-systems, and so forth.

The problem with statements of this sort is with their poor linkage to the practical concerns of teaching. The instructor is involved in a deliberate teaching-learning process, often with students who are very confused about what learning means. This involvement tends to obscure the more philosophical considerations in education though the instructor may remain aware of the philosophical role he is playing as he clarifies the subject matter and leads students not just to facts but to a way of thinking about the facts. The biology instructor, for example, cannot help but engage in the philosophy of biology, yet he does not always find a philosophy of biology in educational philosophy.

The philosophy of biology springs from the science of biology but, in turn, leads to a reflection on the role of biological science. Such a connection is demonstrated well in bio-ethics. The sharp increase in genetics research and engineering since the 1950s has caused a change in the subject matter which the community college biology instructor pursues. In his educational role, he cannot divorce himself from the transpiring ethical issues, which is not to say that they become dominant in his presentations. He still is primarily concerned with the transmission of biology as a science. Yet he is aware of how his field influences the development of man's future, not just the future of science. That he can become so engaged is reflected in this concluding statement in a review of genetics research by a community college instructor:

> We thus perceive terrible questions arising from recent scientific developments. Man is directly involved in his own biologic future; therefore the decisions as to that future should be made by an informed society with a clear set of values. [125]

It is fairly easy to draw this analogy. It is much more difficult to make the connections between philosophy and other fields, such as the philosophy of aesthetics and art education, or moral philosophy and the psychology of human development; yet a search for these connections can help to establish a structure of general education. The search is so demanding that it cannot come to fruition from isolated individual pursuit of studies and lesson preparations. Rather; it calls for a continual sharing of experience and dialogue between the disciplines, focused on common themes. As an experience is a whole of the moment, the dialogue need not be aimed at a predetermined result: it has great value in and of itself. It is this dialogue which is at the heart of missions development.

Why do the efforts to build interdisciplinary courses fail? One of the reasons most often cited is the high cost of these efforts. If an interdisciplinary seminar means placing two or three instructors in the same class so that the faculty-student ratio is cut (for example from 30:1 to 10:1) the possibilities of extending this program to a significant portion of the student population are nullified. To be sure, there are other large lecture/small group combinations which permit team-teaching while maintaining FTE ratios, but it is unrealistic to assume that interdiscip-

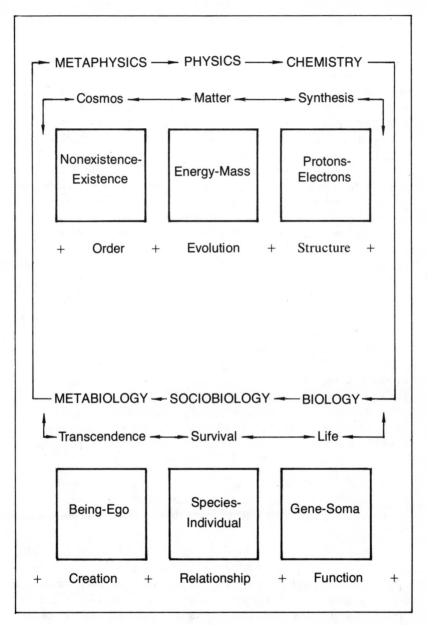

Figure 6.1

Source: Jonas Salk, *The Survival of the Wisest (New York: Harper & Row, 1973)*

linary courses may be enabled by substantially reducing faculty-student ratios.

But is there not another reason for the failure of interdisciplinary courses? They usually begin with the planning of structure rather than with the sharing of knowledge and conceptual approaches. Even the structural considerations are not weighted sufficiently as a research task. There is a tacit assumption that the disciplines can be grafted on to one another. Eventually, cohesiveness might be achieved if fields of knowledge were static. All fields are dynamic, however; by the time a true interdisciplinary outline of subject matter is resolved, rather than just an alternation of the disciplinary units, the state of knowledge has advanced. This problem is particularly keen in the introduction of the social sciences, where the need to forge relationships is the greatest, and in the introduction of the physical sciences aimed at showing the connections between science and technology. It should be less of a problem in the humanities.[126] (The state of the humanities represents another kind of problem in general education; see the concluding section.)

Rather than the *a priori* construction of interdisciplinary courses, there is a *trans-disciplinary* approach to the problem of general education through a search for the "philosophies-of" the disciplines.[127] This search inevitably leads to a perspective on the place of the disciplines in a broader context of the contemporary sciences as a whole. Through philosophical inquiry, as distinguished from the old variety of educational philosophy, the common ends of the disciplines and the ways in which they might reflect each other become more ascertainable. An example of trans-disciplinary thinking along these lines is provided by Salk in the following model.[128] (See **Figure 6.1**)

The Salk model may or may not be useful for promoting a dialogue between the disciplines. It illustrates again, however, that the relationships between the sciences and philosophy can be considered holistically.

There is a need also to consider the practical means by which these dialogues may be initiated. Before turning to this matter, however, there is another mode that deserves to be investigated: a trans-disciplinary approach is implicit in any attempts to study the future consequences of present developments and alternative courses of action.

110

Futures Study

Though it sometimes is allowed to become an ideological backwash, a serious debate has been going on for the past few years — certainly since the 1973 Arab oil embargo — on America's energy future. The debate cannot focus exclusively on America's future, of course, for the energy equation involves all of the world's resources, therefore rendering energy consumption not only a national problem but a global problem. While this debate has witnessed serious disagreements about the development of alternative energy sources, especially nuclear ones, there is little disagreement that an energy crisis is likely to prevail in the final quarter of this century. The coming of the crisis was foreseen long before the oil embargo. For the past 100 years, American civilization has been built on the easy exploitation of abundant energy resources. But energy is no longer cheap. The problem has profound implications for institutional development as well as for international cooperation and order.

Here, then, is a problem of the present which is being seen in a perspective of the future. (The impact on policy development is another question.) Since it is obviously so basic, the energy shortage problem is perhaps more dramatic, but other problems may be perceived futuristically as well, and as they are, the relationships also become more clear. If general education is to contribute to an understanding of man's problems, the curriculum needs a futuric sense. If general education is structured so as to address futuric themes, the disciplines are so challenged that they must come out of isolation. "America's energy future," for example, taps the physical sciences, biological sciences, technologies, social sciences, and even the humanities if different forms of energy and values are considered.

Unfortunately, futurism has become a fad. Many schools and colleges have introduced courses on the future and, in some cases, even an entire curriculum.[129] These courses could prove to be stimulating, but no structural changes are necessary in the curriculum in order to accomplish a reorientation, nor is it necessary to design new courses on the future (for example, "Sociology of the Future"). Such courses perceived as another discipline could even retrench the case for futures study. The argument is not against curriculum change or course inventions, which may be well justified on other grounds. It is, rather, an argument *for infusing all curricula* with the notion of education as a preparation for the future.

Vast amounts of material are available for this purpose to which virtually all of the disciplines have contributed.[130] "Futures study" is a very general term and, by itself, doesn't mean much, but the exploration of the future and the search for ways to influence its direction are not just a fad.[131] Centers for the study of the future now are operative at several universities, and there are numerous such professional organizations in the United States and Europe. (A clearing-house is the World Future Society in Washington, D.C.) Briefly defined, "Futures study" has three main characteristics: (1) it aims at improving data bases for policy-making and long-term planning; (2) it employs a "systems approach", and (3) it aims at sensitizing institutions and raising the awareness of *possible alternative futures*. Whatever its limitations, at least it forces an acknowledgement that the old, fatalistic view of the future as something inevitable, fixed, and unforeseeable is undeserving and even irresponsible.

There is, of course, a danger of misrepresenting or confusing what futures fields are all about. The faddist distortions are seen in "predictions" and those linear projections about more and more material objects and things to tickle people's fancies. There is also much controversy and disagreement among those who participate formally in the work of forecasting or conjecturing about the future. Most "futurists" (many of whom would disavow the name) would agree that, while the assessment of alternative futures is a legitimate activity if it stems from a data base, the future cannot be predicted. Daniel Bell also points out that there is no such thing as "the future"; reasonably, we can speak only of the future of education, the future of government, and so forth. Perhaps all forecasts of the future ought to be taken with a grain of salt. As they are examined, there is sometimes a tendency to measure the present solely against the projected conditions, forgetting that the present is a creation of the past and that the valuation process, which should be the heart of the study, must take into account past, present, and future. Without this sense of time reverberating, the examination is shunted too easily into ideologies, which are as futile in their own way as the blind waiting for whatever is going to happen, to happen.

Human decisions do contribute to the determination of human future conditions. For the student, an absorbing question is, "What is my future going to be like?" If this question is to be taken seriously in general education, the themes must be both humanistic and futuric. Humanistic education confronts the student with the problem of self-knowledge and turns it into a recognition that he or she does indeed have value-choices to make. Yet individual futures are not totally self-determined. Futuric education should illustrate concern for the future of society in the making and lead the student not only to an understanding of his or her institutions but to a perspective on change. In the ideal sense, there is an attempted fulfillment of Arnold's desire to teach students "to see life steadily and to see it whole."

Some Practical Considerations

How are these aims to be accomplished when we ourselves are lacking in self-knowledge and a holistic perspective? Clearly, as educators, we do not have sufficient wisdom for a full accomplishment of general education. There is little hope that the struggle for a revitalization will be won through some ingenious structural reform or philosophical stroke that no one has thought of before. Yet, though we live in the Country of the Blind, the struggle may go on if we transcreate the spirit of learning through group endeavors outside of the classroom. General education can become adventurous by such example.

The first practical consideration is to select themes for the convening of the disciplines within major areas of concentration. Academic divisions (or other such administrative clusters) are created for this purpose, which therefore should be high on every division's agenda. These themes become materials for co-curricular and community education planning. A central committee on staff development, perhaps with the aid of a total faculty survey, then may select from the assortment of division activities and interests those subject matters which are a concern inter-divisionally for the sponsorship of all-college conferences and in-service workshops. Thus, there are created at least two levels of academic dialogue, which may fuse at certain points.

Some coordination is necessary, of course. This can be achieved through the planning of an activities calendar. Depending on the college's organizational structure, there may be three planning groups involved in calendar coordination: (1) staff development committee, (2) co-curricular activities committee, and (3) community education committee. If a cooperative sense of the equal importance of these three areas prevails, the dovetailing of resources may be effected as the committee representatives look constantly for those activities which may be enjoined. Every community, for example, has individuals and groups who may contribute to and benefit from professional conferences. It is in the faculty's self-interest to establish better relationships with the community, and it is obviously a college interest to do so.

Therefore, few, if any, conferences should be closed to the community. The objective should be to bring community representatives into the conferences as direct participants.

A sophisticated degree of coordination raises genuine possibilities of credit extension for participation. Credit extension to students assumes that the conference and workshop themes are related to curriculum concerns and are backed up by reading or research assignments. Credit extension to faculty in the form of Continuing Education Units assumes, of course, that a policy exists which stipulates hours of attendance (for example, 10 hours per C.E.U.)

Academic activities at the division level are likely to be primarily informal. The college activities calendar should be consulted in the scheduling of any formal events (for example, visiting lecturers). On the other hand, the occurrence of impromptu events should not be stifled. If there is a high degree of personal investment in the values of academic dialogue, the coordination will not always be smooth.

What are the trans-disciplinary themes? Some examples already are provided in the preceding sections. Others can be developed from among many possibilities: for example, the communications revolution, which includes information theory, linguistics, the role of the computer, and mass media; world population and resources (the world food problem); energy, ecology, and economics; evolution, social movements, and the idea of progress; man, science, and technology; heredity, environment, and personality development; science and religion; the pure languages of mathematics and music; education and health care; adult development and the human potential movement; community development and work force needs; and remedial instruction in all curricula. A Delphi inquiry (see Documentation, No. 28) might be useful in selecting and firming up themes perceived to be the most relevant and controversial. Controversy, while stimulating, is not sought for its own sake, but to promote the full exercise of different ways of looking at a problem. Faculty will disagree, of course, in the presence of students and others. How can such confusion lead to integration? Beneath the structure are values of integrity and mutual respect among peers to be demonstrated in the search for knowledge. Without this synergic command, the whole enterprise falls apart.

A second major practical consideration relates to missions development. Organization by departments or divisions is the norm in community colleges; these arrangements are administratively useful and provide for an exchange of views between colleagues on course development. However, they also contribute to the isolation of the disciplines. In addition to departmental organization, there is a need for interdisciplinary team development according to the curricula with which the faculty members are primarily involved. For example, the technology curriculum may include general education courses such as sociology and English composition. The route to better integration of these courses, with the curriculum objectives as they are designed and reviewed, is better laid if the instructors of these courses meet regularly with the technology faculty on curriculum matters. The humanities, especially, have this additional burden. A large college with a philosophy department might even consider the assignment of philosophy instructors to separate divisions as primary. The entire humanities faculty might be separated periodically in this manner, rejoining occasionally during the separation for administrative purposes but spending most of their time on another mission development. There is less justification for doing so in the social sciences, where the disciplines change faster, but the same exchange principles apply.

Through the resulting dialogue, experimental interdisciplinary courses then might develop with a more purposeful base. For example, a course on "Man and Technology" (stressing impacts of technological development and engineering systems) could be the key element in the general education component of a technology curriculum if the humanities faculty member were supplementing through a well-grounded critique rather than just adding on to the curriculum pattern. The following diagram (**Figure 6.2.**) illustrates a model that might be achieved. The relational functions are assumed in the Man and Technology course.

"Man and Technology" is an exciting course for its instructors because, in addition to practical observation, it requires general scholarship. It is but one example which seems to place the responsibility of general education mission development on "Liberal Arts" faculty. Its success, however, obviously depends upon strong support from the technology faculty. Since general education is not likely to be revitalized through exclusive dependence on the old Liberal Arts base, attention also needs to be given to the role of the faculty associated with "career programs." What practical skills can be developed through general education? If the future should require a significant change of life styles, is there a creative role for the technology faculty, for example, in the offering of maintenance and recycling courses? Or, perhaps even more vital, what general education possibilities are emerging from

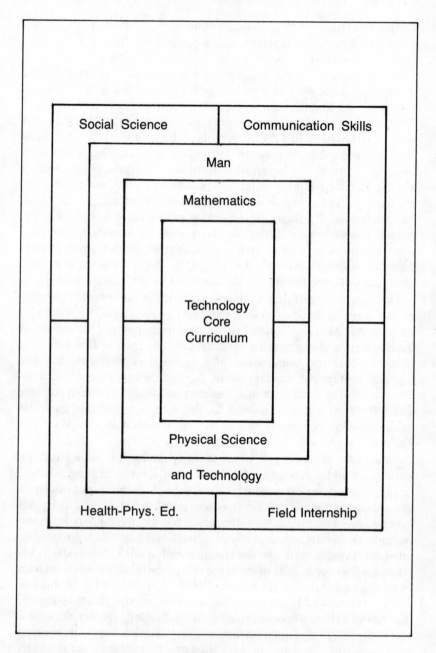

Figure 6.2

allied health curricula? In a more organic approach to the relationships of man and technology, which focus less absolutely on the specialization and professionalization of human welfare protection, are there basic courses in preventive and emergency medical care, home health, or nutrition which may be delivered as an aspect of general education?

"Man and Technology", therefore, is only a metaphor to be used in the broader challenge of fostering general education through general scholarship. In conclusion, some random comments are offered on this topic.

General Scholarship

The future of general education in the community college is linked with the future of staff development programs. Without vigorous moves to establish solid programs aimed at professional growth, the decline of the community college may be as rapid as its rise. These programs must stimulate general scholarship. Like most aspirations, general scholarship involves risk. It means taking chances on others, trusting that they are capable of responding instructively to ideas and probes into their areas. In a non-synergic climate, there is sometimes a mood of individual competence that encases like a shell. The individual claims, "I know what I'm doing, but those idiots in the next building do not." It is also a shell of protection. A well-qualified faculty brings to the college a remarkable array of talents and interests, but unless there is willingness to share them outside of the classroom and office confines, these talents and interests are apt to lie fallow. True competence is matched with self-confidence; confidence in the community comes by exchange. This exchange depends on approaching the disciplines with considerably less awe than community college faculty have felt in the past.

The state of general education is such that a breakthrough to transdisciplinary modes has become imperative. It is only inurement and a provincial fear that prevents it. Boldness of thematic presentation is not a transgression of scholarship so long as the notion of expertise is carefully avoided and the individual strives for relationships to his discipline, which remains the base of his perspective. As an "explainer of knowledge" rather than an original discoverer, the community college instructor should enjoy the sapiential authority necessary for this work. It requires a sense of identity as a professional educator and a willingness to bend to the hard but rewarding tasks of general scholarship.

117

Freed from discipline barriers, sociology faculty may look beyond sociology (as the best sociologists always have done) to the entire educational community of the college and, thereby, to whatever activities and concepts can be found through colleagues that will help in the task of explaining the nature of human organization. (The relief from the terminological abstraction of sociology papers should in itself, be welcome). "But one must be careful." Of course! Errors of interpretation are possible, likely even; but this very awareness is a check. If the community college instructor, as a generalist, is honest, he can survive the mistakes. The point is that, through general search, he is constantly broadening as well as deepening his perspective. It is this perspective on knowledge that brings life to general education. Maslow said it well: facts do not just lie there "like oatmeal in a bowl"; they require interpretation. Errors can be corrected and honestly announced. Students will not be so permanently injured as they are by the old strait-jacket approach to subject-matter.

The humanities faculty in any community college have a unique opportunity to demonstrate the relevance of general scholarship in all of the college's missions and to play a strong leadership role in the revitalizing of general education. As the humanities are currently focused and organized, however, it is doubtful that this opportunity can be exploited. This comment is not intended to be polemical. It springs partly from a view of the empty themes of despair — human suffering without hope — which are conveyed in so much of the current subject matter. The fascination with the "Kosinski school" of art precludes a stronger role in valuation because, if it is true that the world is only a constant nightmare, there is nothing left but to follow the most extreme sensations. There is no place for rationality, because rationality fails completely. Students may be attracted to this theme, as they are attracted to Dracula movies, but if the world may be truly seen only through cynical eyes, why does the mask of cynicism fall away in the face of genuinely valiant belief? The future may try men's bodies and souls as much as has the past, but the humanities tradition shows that men endure and prevail and constantly seek redemption.

But there is also an organizational problem in the humanities, resulting from past patterns in higher education that combine the teaching of literature and English composition. It may be important to the future of general education, and in the faculty's self-interest which is tied to that future, to break this pattern completely. The English writing instructor's role in general education is not an envious one, but it obviously is growing in importance. Long hours of applying a red pencil to student papers are drudgery for any instructor. To make the work more effective requires coordination and support in all curricula which the English faculty must generate. To give new eminence to writing skills instruction also requires strong administrative support for professional development activities and the commitment of resources which will encourage the English faculty's focus on its primary assignment of skills development and their college-wide leadership to cement this purpose. Such leadership might even entail writing skills workshops for other faculty as well as for students, for it is clear that faculty themselves need the instruction. (Can this problem be faced honestly?)

The sciences also have a stake in general scholarship. The biology faculty, for example, may find value in looking at what the social sciences are doing. A strong case could be made for general biology and cultural anthropology as the most fundamental courses in a general education program. Add to these courses humanistic psychology, history of science, philosophy of ethics and aesthetics, and basic principles of economics and geography for the core of a new liberal arts curriculum while maintaining, of course, the emphasis on reading and writing skills development. But, here, the argument begins to falter. Such courses are mere personal preferences if they are not related to the whole curriculum endeavor. Well taught, a course in mythology or mass media could be just as valuable. The challenge is not to select the "right courses" — though it seems fair to say that some courses are more basic than others — but to forge the entire curriculum through a constant valuing process that gets it out of the classroom into the greater community.

Community college faculty have performed many small miracles with students in their classrooms and laboratories. In the future, community education is likely to call for different kinds of responses. The invention of new conceptual frameworks for community education may depend on general scholarship and general education even more than occupational programs do. For example, a strand on "the future of the community" might be fashioned by borrowing modules from general education courses. This view does not imply that science should be taught on street corners, but it does suggest that resiliency and ability to generalize in meaningful ways within a shortened time frame will be valued — and valuable — instructional commodities. Resiliency is important because not all first efforts in community-based instruction go well. Moreover, community programs cannot be planned and prepared for far in advance, but must be tailored to local needs as these needs are identified.

The new emphasis on community education is a reminder that, at the community college level, knowledge is not pursued for its own sake. Men do not live in knowledge; they live in environments. To discover those environmental conditions — physical, aesthetic, social, and moral — which promote man's intrinsic values is a transdisciplinary, unifying task. To enhance understanding of the results of that inquiry is the most noble aim of general education. Concluding this examination of values and the future, a personal interpretation of the philosophical quest is offered in the final chapter.

Summary

Hypotheses are presented on an emerging new world view. They include reference to the social context of science, the shift to holistic approaches, syntheses of philosophy and science, the legitimization of parapsychology, and active concern for the future. It is suggested that this new view has been developing in many different fields and that it has great significance for education. Practical reasons for placing new emphasis on general education are evident in work force realities and continuing specialization which builds job obsolescence into industrial organization. More philosophical reasons concern technology and human values. The most important questions for community college faculty facing the issues of general education are: "What should be taught?" and "How can we keep abreast of changing concepts in the academic fields?" Several propositions are made, including the need for employing general philosophy and futures study as transdisciplinary approaches. Practical considerations include planning and coordination and the development of interdepartmental consultation. Most important are the intrinsic values and the confidence brought into the endeavor by the participants. General scholarship required of community college professional staff, especially those involved in general education, is a demanding but rewarding activity. Staff development programs, respectful of faculty differences, are the key to developing a greater understanding of the unique role of community colleges as the new house of general education during the current educational crisis. Attention is turned to the continuing quest for values in the final chapter.

VII

QUEST FOR VALUES

What can be said of the community college as a community prototype that will be commonly accepted as true either in a universal ideal sense or as already active in the behavior system? Perhaps nothing, but rejecting this relativist view and risking for the sake of hope, suggested here are two principles that go to the heart of all community life.

The first is that, believing in our own dignity, we are able to believe in the dignity of others. The second is that all men share a desire for integrity in their lives. Dignity is personal. The notion of integrity may be applied not only to the individual but to elements of the organization and to the organization as a whole; integrity is the striving for authenticity and wholeness. In speaking of his integrity, a man defends his autonomous functioning just as an organization does. A man's dignity, on the other hand, refers to the uniqueness of his personality and his reliance upon it.[132] Though these concepts often are regarded as somewhat vague, they have great value. Neither dignity nor integrity are the same thing as autonomy, the subject of so much philosophical dispute; yet both are related to it. In the end, their acceptance depends on a view of man's autonomy.

Men may speak of the ideal and the reality and the shadow that falls between, just as they may speak of values, knowing at the same time their vulnerability or their inability to curb passion. So it is in discussing dignity and integrity. How, then, can these values be discussed so as to be brought fully into consideration without falling into that trap of "putative intuition" (Wolfe), of moralizing, or even worse, of pontification? Where are the data? What sources can be used?

We have seen through Dewey's eyes the pre-eminence of aesthetic experience in human life and the essentiality of an aesthetic environment for enhancing the "quality of life." We have seen through Maslow's eyes that the hierarchy of human needs includes spiritual values, the intrinsic nature of which should be explored by social science. We have seen in the emergence of a new world view the greater possibility

121

of a trans-disciplinary, holistic approach to man's problems as well as a broadening of the scope of science and a deepening of its power.

Out of these developments, is there sufficient validation of a usable system of values that includes the values of human dignity and integrity? Can we believe in these values because we know that they are true for all men everywhere, so that they do not depend on exhortation or dialectical thinking, so that they are not merely the images of good politics — and so that they are so naturally viable that any organization must be based upon them and measure all actions by their truth? The answer is not easily forthcoming because these are the values, along with others such as freedom, individuality, and privacy, which are officially proclaimed in modern bureaucratic, industrial society. The real values of that society are perhaps more closely tied to production and consumption, but images are sometimes confused with realities. The question, therefore, is first one of values clarification and, ultimately, of universal discovery.

The answer requires a continuing search not only through behavioral science, which has betrayed this search in the past, but through examination of philosophical or metaphysical sources which may reinforce a commonality of understanding. In this search, the philosophy of Immanuel Kant comes to the fore.[133]

Kant's Moral Philosophy

Kant undoubtedly is the foremost moral philosopher since the Reformation. It is interesting that Kant follows not only David Hume, whose moral skepticism he challenged, but also Thomas Hobbes, whose influence on the Founding Fathers was as great as that of the natural rights *philosophes*. For Hobbes, man's fundamental nature was evil and had to be brought under control by the state. The Hobbesian view, reinforced by puritanism, has been an important strand in American political thought and remains alive today, fed no doubt by the testimony of violence and necrophilia which have been so pervasive in the American experience. America is also a product of the Englightenment, however, and the most enlightened philosopher of that age was Immanuel Kant.

Kant, unlike Hobbes, opted for human freedom and growth. For Kant, man's nature contains the seeds of good. In his essay on Education, he said, "Providence has willed, that man shall bring forth for himself the good that lies hidden in his nature, and has spoken, as it were, thus to man: 'Go forth into the world. I have equipped thee with every tendency towards the good. Thy part let it be to develop these tendencies."[134]

The complexity (and, at times, obscurity) in Kant's philosophical writings is revealed, however, by the attention he also gives to the depravity of human nature. Especially in his "Religion Within the Limits of Reason Alone," he recognizes man's propensity to evil as a result of free will, which, for Kant, is a rational power. The conflict of inclinations toward good and evil is described, in part, by such references as "perversity of the heart"[135] or "a certain insidiousness of the human heart which deceives itself in regard to its own good and evil intentions."[136] If man is to be held responsible for his corruption, it must be on the grounds of his original predisposition to good from which he has freely departed. Man *is* free.

Since freedom is a "mere idea", it cannot be illustrated in the laws of nature. Therefore, it cannot be explained: it can only be defended. Freedom *is*, Kant contends, because men have the power of reason. It is through the development of their natural tendencies toward the good that men *earn* their freedom and become worthy of happiness.

Man's good will can be subverted, but the hope of revival is never lost because man has moral consciousness — "the moral law within." Man's morality is based on universal laws and principles, the knowledge of which is *a priori*, that is, it requires no experiental proof: "Moral concepts cannot be obtained by abstraction from any empirical and hence merely contingent knowledge."[137] Human freedom and happiness are exercised by the wedding of knowledge and action toward good ends, which is made possible through inquiry into higher concepts than are revealed by experience alone. For example, all men should tell the truth. The fact that men may tell lies and benefit thereby does not destroy the validity of this universal principle. Though men never may be entirely certain about their motivations and convictions, as they reach fuller understanding of moral concepts through reason, they become obligated by a Categorical Imperative: "Act only on a maxim by which you can will that it, at the same time, should become a universal law."[138]

Such understanding obviously depends upon education (which is therefore, above all, a moral force). "Man can only become man by education. He is merely what education makes of him."[139] Education includes discipline and instruction, the latter being instrumental for supplying men with culture as well as a reflection of culture. Kant distinguishes between discipline and "maxims," which are the proper basis of moral education, noting that discipline is necessary for men because they have the gift of reason which frees them from instinct. Discipline and freedom are juxtaposed. The whole of education provides the nurturance of human growth. A man's natural capabilities are developed by education, while some aspects of culture are only imparted. The ultimate aims of education are the cultivation of the mind (physical culture) and the formation of character (moral culture). Man grows through discipline first, and then through freedom, which nurtures his continuing growth as discipline nurtures the child. (Kant did not associate discipline with punishment.)

Moral education is not "moralizing" nor a practice of religious doctrine. Certainly no philosopher has fought harder against dogmatism than Kant. While moral education is based on the process of inquiry, human reason has limits and can never be satisfied totally. The satisfaction of reason is "further and further postponed" by the inquiry process. Nevertheless, man must act. Man's actions may be based on legality or higher law, or may be taken as a universal good — good ends likely to be approved everywhere by every man.

Kant teaches that men are always an end, never merely a means, and should always be treated as such. This "practical imperative" (a powerful form of the Categorical Imperative previously discussed) gives man *dignity*. The practice of the "ends" principle depends upon the condition of morality. Here, in Kant's description of the moral environment, the value of human dignity is honestly asserted:

> In the realm of ends everything has either a price or *dignity*. Whatever has a price can be replaced by something else which is *equivalent*; whatever is above all price, and therefore has no equivalent, has *dignity*. Whatever is related to the general inclinations and needs of mankind has a market price; whatever answers, without presupposing a need, to a certain taste, that is, to pleasure in the mere purposeless play of our emotions has a *fancy price*. But that which constitutes the condition under which alone anything can be an end in itself has not merely a relative value or price, but has an intrinsic value; it has *dignity*.

> Morality is the sole condition under which a rational being can be an end in himself, since only then can he possibly be a law-making member of the realm of ends. Thus only good morals and mankind, so far as it is capable of it, have dignity. Skill and diligence in work have a market price; wit, lively

124

imagination and whims have a fancy price; but faithfulness to promise, good will as a matter of principle, not as a matter of instinct, have an intrinsic value. Neither nature nor art has anything which, if dignity were lacking, they could put in its place . . . The word *respect* alone offers a fitting expression of the esteem in which a rational being must hold it.[140]

Intrinsic values cannot be described in the social order; they are postulated through moral reasoning. On similar grounds in Kant's moral philosophy, legality and ethics are subsumed. In Kant's view, right actions are not sufficient. It is not that right actions have no moral worth, but that only actions taken in knowledge and understanding lead to ethical conduct. In ethical matters, man ought to choose virtue not merely from inclination, but from duty which is defined by Kant thus: "Duty is the necessity of an action, resulting from respect for the law."[141] (As already noted, the law may be juridical or moral.) A man is ethical in the performance of his duty, in other words, not because he performs certain actions but because he knows that he ought to perform them. He has absorbed into his autonomous will a practice based on ethical principles. It is in this sense that we may speak of a person's *integrity*. Beyond the individual, Kant warned against the state which seeks "to establish through force a polity directed to ethical ends" because such action "achieves the very opposite of ethical polity" and thereby undermines the integrity of the state.[142]

In his essay on Enlightenment, Kant explains that integrity may be undermined by self-imposed immaturity. He defines immaturity as "the incapacity to use one's intelligence without the guidance of another."[143] He further explains that what is called "irrationality" has its "reasons" buried beneath layers of ignorance, yet these reasons also are part of the autonomous make-up. Immaturity prevents their discovery and thus conflicts with a sense of integrity. He sees evidence of this immaturity primarily in matters of religion; but again relating to the whole of human endeavor, Kant's linking immaturity to loss of integrity is implicit in his view of statutes and formulas which are allowed to become "mechanical tools" and thus "are the ankle-chains of a continuous immaturity."[144]

Kant's moral writings contribute not only to a greater understanding of values but to the search for values which leads ultimately to the question of man's relationship to God. In all matters of morality, it is not what God forbids that shines through in Kant, despite older popular notions to this effect. "God wills only what is good, and desires that we may love virtue for its own sake, and not merely because He requires it."[145] In other words, God desires not the good but that man *choose* the good.

In the Kantian system, the idea of God is a heuristic concept: pure reason neither can prove nor disprove God's existence; rather, it is a "postulate of practical reason." In other words, reason cannot be extended to an explanation of the spiritual world, that is, the ideal world which transcends experiences (in Kant, the "noumenal" existence.) However, the will is greater than reason. Man's free will and moral consciousness lead to the belief in God, and, indeed, such belief is indispensable to morality. Thus, Kant reversed the standard religious doctrine: rather than moral codes being derived from God, belief in God flows from the moral consciousness. On this basis, universality is obtained.

If God did not exist, the Kantian moral framework would fall apart. However, God exists. The live personal meaning is better left to each man's search. As man moves into God's wilderness, he falls short again and again, yet if he grows thereby, the growth potential is heightened more. God may be hidden in the affairs of men, yet somehow He works in these realms. Kant made it possible for men to reflect better on God's existence and their own moral foundations.

In today's world, Kant may seem to be the distant philosopher. Yet, given the values-crisis which confronts our society, he may have a new importance. If rootlessness and loss of spiritual authority are traceable to cultural relativism and the absence of the key God-question, Kant suggests the possibility of affirmatives. The naturalistic approach to valuation seems more current, but Kant helps to remind us that moral philosophy has wrestled with the problem of values longer than has modern social science.

There is much in Kant, of course, that is challenged by modern empirical science and particularly by the behaviorist school of psychology, which has tended to dominate educational institutions for the past quarter century.[146] Major contentions develop over Kant's epistemology which includes *a priori* knowledge and reference to universal laws and principles as well as his arguments for the existence of God. Existentialism and humanistic psychology pose another challenge to the Kantian moral framework and do so, as we have seen, with strong orientation to human values. The purpose here is not to examine these dichotomous viewpoints, though such examination is well in accord with Kant's method of inquiry, but merely to acknowledge their importance to the practical dialogues which go on in search of values, that is, what men make out of philosophy.

Normative Values

There is evidence in the works of several contemporary thinkers of Kant's lasting influence and the validity of continuing to explore his wisdom. At the same time, later social thinkers, responding to a technology-driven history, remind us of depths and varieties of human experiences not fully plumbed in Kant's philosophy. *Kant is not sufficient*. Other world philosophies have emerged that seem more plausible. Dewey, for example, illustrates a greater respect for the interaction learning process of the empirical social world. Perhaps this difference accounts for the greater attractiveness of Dewey's aesthetic philosophy. Yet, in the assessment of modern social science directions, knowledge of Kant seems essential for a reflective background.

Reliance upon Kant as a philosophical source is valid only as it causes one to reflect on the current misdirections of society and the plight of educational institutions as they seek to gain a values perspective in keeping with the needs of a new morality. Granted, there is danger in eclectic attempts to forge an educational values perspective, but there is perhaps greater danger in adhering to narrow disciplines which, despite their success in specialized discovery, have not contributed to a unified general education.

Where, specifically, do we find connections between philosophy and science in recent research on man and society to indicate the convergence of the disciplines while, at the same time, discovering grounds for the substantiation of intrinsic or *normative* values? A starting point is Maslow's theory of the hierarchy of needs, including self-esteem and self-actualization. Maslow believed that valuelessness — "the ultimate disease of our time" — was related to the concept that nothing transcends culture. His approach to values was scientific, but his conclusions reinforce the case for normative values.

Cultural anthropology contributes further affirmation in the discovery of the tendency of all societies to institutionalize and in the identification of values such as survival, avoidance of suffering, courage, kinship, and child-rearing within all cultures. Without reviewing the work of Lévi-Strauss, it is relevant to point out its fundamental importance, which is that it reveals, beneath the appearance of cultural relativity and non-rational beliefs and practices, underlying structures which are common in all societies. His work on the structures of kinship, for example, shows that the values of exogamus marriage, based on exchange of women as the means of maintaining group life, and the prohibition of incest as a social rule which prevents a biological family from becoming a closed system, are "permanent functional values" universally established.[147]

Granted, these are insufficient grounds for proving that values such as dignity and integrity are indeed normative, but it is first necessary to see that all valuation is not merely subjective expression and that value theories which hold that values only may be described are being severely tested. Once through this obstacle of dominant relativism, the validity of postulating normative values, as Kant did through moral reasoning, is established. This postulation is seen in general systems theory.

General systems theory encompasses both science and philosophy. Principles are postulated on the philosophy end of the spectrum and move toward scientific formulization at the other end.[148] By this continuum, values are included in the scientific formulization. According to Laszlo, who reiterates Maslow, there is always a fusion of facts and values in human systems, for it is the human being who makes the facts dynamic through perceptions and interpretations. In all living systems, whether the system is a simple one, taken from nature, or highly complex, like man, values are built into the system's existence, and there is a norm expressed by all systems in their constant adaptation to their environments. (See Chapter Four, Growth and Adaptation.)

In man's social systems, other normative values, some having been discovered, also may be postulated. However, it is through scientific inquiry that credence is given to these postulations. There are dangers of introducing ethnocentricities and ephemerality on the one hand and sophisticated analysis of trivial questions on the other if there is not a balanced concern for philosophical rigor and scientific inquiry.[149] The use of informed scientific theories on physical man and nature (and the relationship between) is central in the quest for understanding. At the same time, lest it be surmised that the argument implies a steady moving through science to an explanation of the whole of man — as though the soul itself could be scientifically dissected — there are limits to science in a stand-alone capacity.

It follows that what one looks for in the search for values as a meaningful task of general education are those patterns of substantiation over time in both moral philosophy and modern social science.

Maslow, for example, is well substantiated by other contemporary humanistic thinkers, and there is growing anthropological evidence that self-fulfillment is the end of purposeful human endeavor. Maslow's ends also are verified by Kant before him, even though Kantian philosophy does not "belong" in the same world view as that of humanistic psychology. Kant strengthens not only belief in, but knowledge and understanding of, "intrinsic and instinctoid" values. There could be little disagreement between Kant and Maslow on dignity and integrity. They disagree on telic explanations — Maslow staying with nature (even in his description of "peak experiences"), as does most general systems theory.

A further synthesis along these lines is found in the works of Ernest Becker. First, Becker supports Maslow's needs hierarchy, though in a different way, by noting that a basic law of human life is the "urge to self-esteem . . . The crucial function of culture is to make continued self-esteem possible: to provide the individual with the conviction that he is an object of primary value in a world of meaningful action."[150] Becker does not agree readily that man has intrinsic norms, but he may be representative of a renewed effort, found in Kant and perhaps inspired by the work of Teilhard de Chardin (though, curiously, in all his analysis, Becker does not mention Teilhard), to achieve a synthesis of knowledge of nature, body, and soul. If so, there is perhaps, in the end, an even stronger ground for postulating normative values. Therefore, let us explore Becker's views further.

Becker's Synthesis

Becker and Laszlo agree that man's complex value systems are *descriptive* rather than normative. Normative values may be realized only as the conditions of man's fulfillment are created. We might conclude that, in faithfulness to the Enlightenment, as defined by Kant, the creation of such conditions depends on freed intelligence, grounded in the scientific method but respectful of the limits of reason, and on a wide range of opportunities for individual ethical action within human organization. Becker reflects this spirit in his view that value relativity exists where man lacks scientific knowledge of his world but that value relativity shrinks as "man begins operating experimentally under . . . a theory that includes a criticism of major social institutions."[151] The possibilities for reasoned action then are much broader.

The relative value of human sacrifice may be cited to support Becker's argument. In some past societies, this seemingly barbaric practice was for centuries a religious rite deemed essential for crop fertilization and bountiful harvest or to ensure that spring would come again. In some cases, the sacrificial victims were regarded as deities prior to their horrible death. It was only as the influence of Western science spread that this "dark" practice began to be abandoned. Man's hope still lies in his power of reason to assess those forces and structures which constrict his full development and thereby the development of a normative values system.

But wait. As true as this hope may seem, Becker also shows us that the dilemma of man's life is so great that it is only partly true, for, in the generations since Kant, there has been an explosion of knowledge — a body of knowledge now so vast that it is unmeasurable — yet the human condition has not changed. The ritual practice of human sacrifice thus is not so different from modern heroic attempts to avert death and, in the struggle for immortality, to commit even greater forms of evil. In Becker's perspective, the universal fear of death generates evil even as it motivates the will to overcome evil. Thus, man is unable "to approach the problem of human evil from the side of psychology."[152] History since the Enlightenment has taught us the weakness of rationalism in that it did not fully understand human nature. Becker asks, "What are we going to improve if men work evil out of the impulse to righteousness and goodness?"[153] The dilemma is indeed confounding.

Becker's view wavers as his analysis progresses, as though it were not quite completed. His last work delimits the hope which is expressed in his earlier writings as he focuses on the problem of evil through psycho-historical analysis, but a theme which remains constant is that a transcendent force may be found in the merger of science and religion. "The heart of a science of man would be half empirical and half ideal — precisely the point at which it merges logically with religion."[154] While it is questionable as to how much faith Becker had, in the end, in man's evolutionary capacity for a transcendence, this theme demands continuing exploration. In the view of Teilhard: "Religion and science are the two conjugated faces or phases of one and the same act of complete knowledge — the only one which can embrace the past and future of evolution so as to contemplate, measure and fulfill them."[155]

Becker's earlier analysis educes organization prototypes which elevate the concept of community and its contribution to autonomy in place of alienation. He first establishes the problem of heroism in modern life: "How does the dignity, control, bearing, talent, and duty of my life contribute to the fuller development of mankind, to life in the cosmos?[156] In a later work, he cites the influence of Kant in phrasing the Enlightenment concept of community and goes on to the philosophy of Buber and Royce, which focused on the intergrowth of loyalty and community.[157] Becker then takes loyalty and community one step further in his conclusion of the ultimate need: "Maximum support for one's new self can only come from a community of free men centered in God."[158] The God-centered community is one in which each individual orients himself to a *sustaining source of power*."[159] Without this power to lean on, man is helpless and alone; whatever the power chosen goes far to determine his basic outlook on life. (This same thought is perhaps the essence of the proverb, "As a man *thinketh in his heart*, so is he.")

In our reliance on the scientific method, we may fail to recognize that pre-scientific knowledge grasped just as well the basic problems of man. Lévi-Strauss helps to remove these blinders in his discussions of primitive man's intelligence, which was no less than our own. Religion once explained the world totally; the totality of that view was no more or less limitative and codified than the scientific view of reality. Becker understood the place for a religious critique on why man is not experiencing a fuller humanity. He saw the betrayal and false- profoundness in behaviorist psychology with its manipulative suggestions.

He also saw that the driving force behind the mystery of life "includes more than reason alone."[160] Becker's analysis shows that he was engulfed by the enormity of the problem of evil; yet he leads us to greater truth in his revelations that evil is not instinctive but an organismic condition, and that, in a scientific social theory — neither conservative nor radical —, man's aggressive and destructive impulses may be objectively assessed in the design of non-destructive community.

Still, Becker lacks the fullness of Teilhard's spiritual insight. He does not recognize the separateness and miraculousness of a spiritual reality by which men, tapping into it, may be genuinely lifted out of alienation and transformed. Nor does he seem to grant full measure to that individualistic propensity of men to risk greatly, sometimes even death, for what is not survival nor escape from evil but spiritual achievement through that "primal and universal psychic energy" (Teilhard) existing of itself. There is at least a fleeting suggestion of the power of love as greater than the power of death in Becker's analysis, but his view is that the latter is central in all ideologies and heroic struggles to the present time. Man, he implies, is far less fascinated by love than by death. Yet his analysis of the structure of evil gives hope of a continued analysis, which, combined with the religious ideal of godliness, raises the possibility of a new birth of hope: synthesis of scientific knowledge and spiritual understanding as the guiding light of a pluralistic community. This synthesis includes the postulation of values that, universally realized, could overcome alienation and militant aggressiveness — perhaps the last hope.

The mystery of God and man's destiny are beyond science, but man is forever the heroic creature who cannot relinquish hope and goes on following a crooked spiritual path. Becker recognized social sciences' hesitation to use the word "God" or other Leibnizian words like "soul", "mysticism," or "cosmic consciousness", but he believed that, when man begins to feel comfortable "with insights that both poets and scientists share," such words will be more readily used in the quest for understanding.[161] Becker is right: the word "God" can have poignant meaning to unbelievers as well as believers, and surely no more fundamental question can be undertaken in general education than that of God's existence. (Fortunate, indeed, is the community college with philosophy professors who know how to approach it.) As Becker concludes, "We are now in a position to see that these kinds of constructs — meaning, conviction, sense of intimacy with the cosmic process — must be *at the very center* of a science of man in society."[162]

These works from Kant to Becker deepen our understanding of the tragedy in the human condition. They also serve to reduce skepticism and cynicism, the greatest eroders of the human spirit. Yet, the human condition may be such that man cannot escape suffering and alienation except as he finally finds God. It may be that, for all his efforts, the books cannot be balanced except in after-life (the probability of which is made immensely more ascertainable by the work of Moody and Kubler-Ross.) Human efforts, however, need not be trivial even in microcosm. All of Western philosophy has dealt with the concept of community and its associated values. Community and loyalty and integrity and dignity and love — if these are worthwhile new starts must be made somewhere, even in so small a place as the community college.

The Energies of Love

Some day, after we have mastered the winds, the waves, the

tides, and gravity, we shall harness for God the energies of
love: and then, for the second time in the history of the world
. . . man will have discovered fire.

— Teilhard de Chardin

How love enters into community college evaluation and development
is not clear and not to be modeled, but this final comment is offered in
the belief that it does belong somewhere in the interstices of all evaluation and development systems.

However near or far one travels to meet people, the love-and-death
struggle in human affairs is apparent. It does not require philosophy or
social science to be emerged as a theme, which is why there is another
dimension to the new world view that is not based on scientific method.
A human potential movement is unfolding of tremendous strength that
is not completely defineable in rational terms. In fact, it seems to have
significant antirational aspects, so that it is sometimes explained as
"last-ditch" romanticism. It is seen, too, as a drive for an increasingly
sensate culture. It also may be a yearning of people for security,
something to hold on to, in a restless, chaotic world. However it is
labeled, the movement seems genuine. It accounts for the explosion of
interest in meditation, mind control, transactional analysis, primal
therapy, sexual therapy, the occult, psychic phenomena, and it is seen
in a great religious revival. While it no doubt carries some dangers and
negative influences, a spiritual awakening is manifested which, despite
its variety of forms, holds the promise of a retrenchment of those
impersonal forces generated by rapid technological change. Which
forms will emerge triumphant in the main is unclear, but there is hope
that it will find distillation in a greater doctrine of love.

To speak of "love" as doctrine seems controverting, for, in the ideal
sense of *agapé*, it transcends all doctrines; and, where it is expressed as
an institutional claim, it can lead to intolerance, or in a milder form, to
condescension that outweighs the proclaimed love in its attack on
integrity. Thus, narrow adherence to any one of these forms of personal
search as the "only way" negates the possibility of their coalescense to
the end of mature love. Yet the world has been influenced by men, those
fully self-actualized individuals who have made love a creative doctrine. Socrates, Jesus, Gandhi immediately come to mind. Such lives
result continually in a new birth of heroism. We fail to follow their
examples because our institutions have not yet opened the way to
similar self-actualization. In commenting on the life of Jesus, Keats

lamented that his mind and words and greatness had been devitalized by institutionalization: "Yet through all this I see his splendor."[163]

To love begins as a matter of choice. The average American male following his competitive drives does not even begin to understand until middle-age, by which time it is difficult to estimate how much damage he has done or the guilt that haunts him. For this reason, if for no other, "women's liberation," an institutional form of the human potential movement, is actually co-liberating. Maslow pointed out how poverty-stricken most social theories are in their reference to "love" yet how crucial love is to self-esteem and self-actualization. In the past, it has been seen almost as a weakness in our cultural perspective even to discuss such concepts. Fortunately, corrections are being made. Young people today understand better. In their celebrations and camaraderie, they reflect a natural openness to love. Much personal anxiety and confusion are seen there, too, of course. But the point has been well made that, whereas older generations are able only to intellectualize on "brotherhood," the younger generation seems able to embrace it emotionally as well.

Love is the highest form of synergy. It may be only idle dreaming to postulate that love can be made greater than death and the fear of death. Yet, if man does not blow up his planet first, the next nova point in his evolution may occur as he comes to a fuller appreciation of the energies of love and begins acting in the knowledge that, by love, life is best sustained and moved.

As the community college strives for a perspective on values and the future, it does so as a system within systems. Its values perspective is created accordingly. As a teaching institution, however, it has a unique role in values clarification. What goes on in its offices and classrooms may not be defined as a doctrine of love, perhaps, but even with its necessary toughmindedness, education always has had something to do with sensitizing (or deadening) people's awareness of these realms. Out of a complex, riddled mass of values set against an uncertain future, there still vibrates that challenge of education.

CHECKLIST OF
EVALUATION AND DEVELOPMENT COMPONENTS

A. Master Planning
    Missions Definition
    Support Goals
    Programmatic Goals
    Structural Change/Innovative Goals

B. Programs/Services Evaluation
    Internal Review
    Outside Consultation
    Inter-Institutional Articulation

C. Individual Evaluation
    Faculty
    Administrative Staff

D. Staff Professional Development
    Unit Level
    College Wide

E. OD Intervention
    Group/Systems Development
    Conflict Resolution

F. Structural Review
    Administrative Organization
    Policies and Procedures

G. Contractual Governance
    Collective Negotiations
    Contract Interpretation/Implementation

H. Institutional Research
    Student and Community Needs Assessment
    Outcomes Analysis
    Cost Analysis

I. Accountability Reporting and Public Relations

DOCUMENTATION

CHAPTER I

1. Adapted from model by G.C. Homans, as summarized in Edgar H. Schein, *Organizational Psychology* (Englewood Cliffs, N.J.: Prentice-Hall, 1965), p. 91.

2. Warren G. Bennis, *Changing Organizations* (New York: McGraw-Hill, 1966), pp. 71ff.

3. John Caffrey, "Predictions for the 1970's," *The Future Academic Community: Continuity and Change*, ed. John Caffrey (Washington, D.C.: American Council on Education, 1969), pp. 261-292.

4. Gordon L. Lippitt, *Visualizing Change: Model Building and the Change Process* (Fairfax, Va.: NTL Learning Resources, 1973), p. 11.

5. For a summary of the history and the trans-disciplinary nature of Organization Development, see *The Journal of Applied Behavioral Science*, Vol. 12, No. 1, 1976, particularly the articles by Friedlander and Burke.

The following definition of *organization development* is from James B. Lau, *Behavior in Organizations* (Homewood, Ill.: Richard D. Irwin, 1975): "a planned, managed, systematic process to change the culture, systems, and behavior of an organization, in order to improve the organization's effectiveness in solving its problems and achieving its objectives." (p.2)

6. Lippitt, *op. cit.*, p. 98.

CHAPTER II

7. See Peter F. Drucker, *The Practice of Management* (New York: Harper, 1954). There are some apparent differences between MBO theory as developed by Drucker and behavioral principles and instru-

136

mental methods which characterize current discussions on its relevance to higher education administration. In 1954, Drucker made these comments on philosophical aspects of MBO:

> What the business enterprise needs is a principle of management that will give full scope to individual strength and responsibility, and at the same time give common direction of vision and effort, establish team work and harmonize the goals of the individual with the common weal.

> The only principle that can do this is management by objectives and self-control. It makes the common weal the aim of every manager. It substitutes for control from outside the stricter, more exacting and more effective control from the inside . . . The manager acts not because somebody wants him to but because he himself decides that he has to — he acts, in other words, as a free man. (pp. 135-136)

More recently, Drucker has addressed the problem of application to public sector organizations, explaining some substantive, as opposed to procedural, implications: see Drucker, "What Results Should You Expect? A User's Guide to MBO," *Public Administration Review*, Vol. 36, No. 1 (January/February, 1976), pp. 12-19.

In this chapter, the focus is on MBO practice and applications as presented by those cited. MBO lessons usually also refer to qualifications of a more philosophical nature, but the emphasis is on comprehensive management strategy and objective-setting techniques.

8. Arthur X. Deegan and Roger J. Fritz, *MBO Goes to College* (Boulder: University of Colorado, 1976).

9. George S. Odiorne, *Management by Objectives* (New York: Pitman, 1965), pp. 54-56.

10. Deegan and Fritz, *op. cit.*, p. 119.

11. Robert E. Lahti, *Innovative College Management* (San Francisco: Jossey-Bass, 1973), pp. 56-57.

12. For a fairly characteristic assessment of the viability of MBO for non-profit oriented organizations, see Rodney H. Brady, "MBO Goes to Work in the Public Sector," *Harvard Business Review* (March-April, 1973), pp. 65-74. Brady explains some of the pitfalls of MBO as well as the advantages.

13. Quotation. James L. Hayes, "Memo for Management," *Manager's Forum*, Newsletter (April, 1976), p. 2.

14. See John D. Millett, "Higher Education Management Versus Business Management," *Educational Record*, Vol. 56,No. 4 (Fall, 1975), pp. 221-225. Millett discusses a report of the Academy for Educational Development which concluded that "the two fields are so different as to preclude any useful exchange of management skills." (p. 221) Other social scientists of organization, including Drucker, dispute these contentions.

15. Kenneth Boulding, *Conflict and Defense: A General Theory* (New York: Harper, 1962), p. 307.

16. Letter of John Keats in *The Letters of John Keats*, ed. Maurice Buxton Forman, 4th Ed. (London: Oxford University Press, 1952), p. 315.

17. Amitai Etzioni, *Modern Organizations* (New York: Prentice-Hall, 1964), p. 16.

18. *Ibid.*, p. 17.

19. This argument may be perceived as a form of goal displacement. It assumes, however, that a framework exists for relating goal activities. See section on organic planning.

20. Adapted from **Figure No. 14** in Jonas Salk, *The Survival of the Wisest* (New York: Harper & Row, 1973), p.26.

21. Deegan and Fritz, *op. cit.*, p. 15.

22. For an interesting definition of *optimization,* see A. O. Converse, *Optimization* (New York: Holt, Rinehart and Winston, 1972), p. 3.

23. George S. Odiorne, *Management and the Activity Trap* (New York: Harper & Row, 1974), pp. 144ff.

24. Robert D. Melcher. Quoted in William F. Glueck, *Organization Planning and Development* (American Management Association, 1971), p. 10.

25. Glueck, pp. 8-10.

26. Much greater sophistication is given to these models by curriculum theorists. For example, see David E. Barbee, *A Systems Approach to Community College Education* (New York: Auerbach, 1972). How-

ever, it is not clear that the problem of the application of these models in the community college field has been solved. Barbee laments that "No institution is truly employing a systems approach . . . to instruction on an across-the-board basis." (p. 107)

27. For a philosophical critique of behavioral learning systems, see Walter Feinberg, "Behavioral Theory and Educational Policy," *The Philosophical Forum,* Vol. VI, No. 1 (Fall, 1974), pp. 40-55.

28. Obviously, planning must go on. Another approach may be possible through use of the Delphi method, developed by Helmar and Dalkey at Rand Corporation, which retains objectivity in the flow of information but provides for qualitative manipulation and iteration. Delphi panelists are provided with background information and questions or probes which elicit their knowledge and informed opinion. The individual responses are compiled, and the total results are fed back to each panelist, who is asked again to respond to the new probes. In this way, the panelists communicate with each other, but answers are not identified by the individual respondent. Successive rounds are aimed at achieving a consensus. Delphi has been demonstrated to be an effective planning tool.

Chapter III

29. Kanter of Honeywell Information Systems suggests that it takes from three to five years for a management information system to become firmly established. See Jerome Kanter, *Management-Oriented Management Information Systems* (Englewood Cliffs, N.J.: Prentice-Hall, 1972), p. 23.

30. See Jerome A. Mark, "Meanings and Measures of Productivity," *Public Administration Review*, Vol. 32, No. 6, (November-December, 1972), pp. 747-753.

31. See Warren W. Gulko, *A Resource Requirements Prediction Model (RRPM-1): An Introduction to the Model*, TR-19, National Center for Higher Education Management Systems, 1971.

32. See Les Foreman, "Impact of the CAMPUS Model on Decision Processes in the Ontario Community Colleges," *Decision Models in Academic Administration*, ed. Albert C. Heinlein (Kent, Ohio: Kent State University, Center for Business and Economic Research, 1974), pp. 47-64.

33. Bertram M. Gross, "The State of the Nation," in *Social Indicators*, ed. Raymond Bauer (Cambridge, Mass.: MIT Press, 1966), p. 267.

The work of the U.S. Department of Labor in this area since the creation of the National Commission on Productivity in 1970 has resulted in the development of "indicators" for the measurement of productivity in government. These comments are not meant to dispute that progress is being made but that the application to education is fundamentally unsound. For further review, see also Charles Ardolini and Jeffrey Hohenstein, "Measuring Productivity in Federal Government," *Monthly Labor Review* (November, 1974), pp. 13-20.

34. The same statement might be made of cost-effectiveness, but the tendency therein is to emphasize the quantitative aspects, which is misleading.

35. The model presented here is an adaptation for community colleges of a model originally developed by Daniel H. Murray and implemented by Murray and McAllister H. Hull at the State University of New York at Buffalo. The Murray-Hull model became the basis for the Chancellor's official Guidelines for Evaluation of Graduate Programs in the State University of New York (November 30, 1972).

36. Especially useful for an overview are: Terry O'Banion, *Teachers for Tomorrow* (Tucson: University of Arizona, 1972); and a workbook by William H. Bergquist and Steven R. Phillips, *A Handbook for Faculty Development* (Washington, D.C.: Council for Advancement of Small Colleges, 1975). The latter contains several OD exercises as well as various ratings forms.

37. Examples of these ratings systems include: the IDEA system developed by the Center for Faculty Evaluation and Development in Higher Education at Kansas State University; the Grasha-Riechmann Student Learning Styles Questionnaire developed by the Institute for Research and Training in Higher Education at University of Cincinnati; the Instructional Assessment System developed by the Council for the Advancement of Small Colleges, Washington, D.C.

See also, Milton Hildebrand, Robert C. Wilson and Evelyn R. Dienst, *Evaluating University Teaching*, Center for Research and Development in Higher Education, University of California at Berkeley, 1971.

38. The research continues on two questions: (1) Do student ratings

lead to improved instruction?; (2) Is there a relationship between good teaching and student learning? The inconsistency of empirical research has been demonstrated in past studies of teaching effectiveness. For example, most of the studies see positive correlations between good teaching and learning, but not all: see Miriam Rodin and Burton Rodin, "Student Evaluation of Teachers," *Science*, Vol. 177, No. 4055 (September 29, 1972), pp. 1164-1166. This study reported that "good teaching is not validly measured by student evaluations *in their current form*" (italics added). Since then, most of the creative work on systems has been done. It remains to be seen what the research will bring if these new forms are widely used.

39. See Harry Levinson, "Appraisal of What Performance," *Harvard Business Review*, Vol. 54, No. 4 (July-August, 1976), pp. 30ff.

40. See Robert R. Blake and Jane Syrgley Mouton, *The Managerial Grid* (Houston: Gulf, 1968).

41. See Rensis Likert, *The Human Organization: Its Management and Value* (New York: McGraw-Hill, 1967). System 1 management is characterized by endemic lack of trust, rigidity, and covert resistance to goals. System 4 management is characterized by high degree of trust, goals acceptance, and reinforcing motivational influences. See Likert's appendix for the composite profile consisting of 51 items.

Likert makes the interesting observation that, when a company becomes anxious about cutting costs and increasing productivity, there is a tendency to shift toward the authoritarian rigidity of System 1: "i.e.,toward a system which they know from their own observation and experience yields poorer productivity and higher costs." (p. 12) What would cause management under duress to make this shift?

42. John Dewey, *Art As Experience* (New York: Capricorn, 1958), p. 38.

43. *Ibid.*, p. 145.

44. *Ibid.*, p. 54

45. *Ibid.*, p. 199.

46. *Ibid.*, p. 109.

47. *Ibid.*, p. 346.

48. *Ibid.*, p. 345.

49. There are, of course, those alienated and lost individuals who make no such efforts or distinctions as are described here. Their presence with tenure is a special problem greater than that of evaluation. Sadly, they continue to occupy the classroom in a perfunctory manner. Only the very difficult process of termination for cause can remove them.

50. For example, "Student-Reactions to College," an open-ended form, developed by Educational Testing Service.

CHAPTER IV

51. Robert Nisbet, *The Social Philosophers: Community and Conflict in Western Thought* (New York: Thomas Y. Crowell, 1973), p. 388.

52. As indicated in Chapter Two notes, Drucker supplies most of the theoretical basis for MBO and could logically be included with McGregor and Maslow in this discussion as well as with other forerunners, such as Rensis Likert and Chris Argyris. Though their analyses take different shapes, they are united in vision.

53. Douglas McGregor, *The Human Side of Enterprise* (New York: McGraw-Hill, 1960), p. 42.

54. Maslow's theory is becoming well known in education. He described five sets of basic needs, which are physiological, safety, love, esteem, and self-actualization, related to one another and arranged in "a hierarchy of pre-potency." See Abraham H. Maslow, *Motivation and Personality*, Second Edition (New York: Harper and Row, 1970), especially Chapter 4.

55. Abraham H. Maslow, *The Farther Reaches of Human Nature* (New York: Viking, 1971), p. 316.

56. Though the study leading to this section concentrated on Maslow's works, it is not meant to imply that humanistic or Third Force psychology is due to Maslow's influence alone. Fromm, Rogers, Allport, and many others, cited by Maslow, created this movement.

57. Maslow defined *self-actualization* in many ways throughout most of his books. The following is a succinct explanation: "Self-actualizing people are gratified in all their basic needs (of belongingness, affection, respect, and self-esteem). This is to say that they have a feeling of belongingness and rootedness, they are satisfied in their love needs, have friends, and feel loved, they have status and place in life and

respect from other people, and they have a reasonable feelingof worth and self-respect." (*The Farther Reaches of Human Nature*, p. 299.) In an earlier work, he expressed *self-actualization* quite simply as, "what a man *can* be, he *must* be." The term was first coined by Kurt Goldstein.

58. Abraham H. Maslow, *Eupsychian Management: A Journal* (Homewood, Ill.: Irwin-Dorsey, 1965), p. 141.

59. Warren G. Bennis, "The Concept of Organization Health," *General Systems Yearbook*, Vol. 7, 1972, especially p. 277. The *healthy personality* definition is credited to Marie Jahoda: "actively masters his environment, shows a certain unit of personality and is able to perceive the world and himself correctly."

60. Adapted from George C. Homans, *The Human Group* (New York: Harcourt, Brace, 1950). "The more frequently persons interact with one another, the stronger their sentiments for friendship of one another are apt to be." (p. 133) This observation is strongly disputed by Lewis Coser in *The Functions of Social Conflict* (New York: Free Press, 1956). Coser's statement that "an increase in social interaction is likely to bring about an increase of hostility as well as of liking" (p. 63) is part of his dialectical argument that close relationship suppresses conflict, thereby creating tensions. If Homans is not entirely correct, Coser seems to go too far the other way.

61. Abraham H. Maslow, *The Farther Reaches of Human Nature* (New York: Viking, 1971), p. 34.

62. Morton Deutsch, *The Resolution of Conflict: Constructive and Destructive Process* (New Haven: Yale, 1973).

63. Erich Fromm, *The Anatomy of Human Destructiveness* (Greenwich, Conn.: Fawcett, 1973), p. 404.

64. Boulding, *Conflict and Defense: A General Theory,* pp. 305-306.

65. See Chris Argyris, *Integrating the Individual and the Organization* (New York: John Wiley, 1964), p. 115.

66. How to distinguish between "petty" and "real" issues is not clear, but such distinctions are made and necessarily so. At the same time, it should be recognized that an issue felt deeply is never perceived to be petty by the party presenting it. In the early phase of Organization

Development theory, T-Group training was emphasized as a means of dealing with this problem. Unfortunately, it cannot always be handled in an organization; again, one must assume maturity. Perhaps there are guiding measures in the persistence of the issue and numbers of people involved.

67. George T. Lock Land, *Grow or Die: The Unifying Principle of Transformation* (New York: Random House, 1973), p. 14. It should be noted that growth is not interpreted to be progress, which concept moves into critical theories of evolution well beyond the scope of this discussion.

68. *Ibid.*, p. 8.

69. *Ibid.*, p. 48.

70. Ervin Laszlo, "A Systems Philosophy of Values." *Behavioral Science, Vol. 18, No. 4 (July, 1973),* p. 257.

71. Abraham H. Maslow, *Eupsychian Management: A Journal* (Homewood, Ill.: Irwin-Dorsey, 1965), p. 1.
It will be noted that a *beruf* concept is also at the root of the "protestant ethic," but the S-A meaning is, of course, different — more like a poetic calling "to unite my vocation and avocation into one" (Frost), or perhaps "a disposition to seek a shape for life from within himself and not in what he could wrest from others." (Lampedusa)

Chapter V

72. J. Robert Oppenheimer. Quoted in Glenn T. Seaborg, "Public Service and Human Contributions," *Oppenheimer* (New York: Charles Scribner's Sons, 1969), p. 56.

73. Everett C. Ladd and Seymour M. Lipset, "The Growth of Faculty Unions," *Chronicle of Higher Education*, January 26, 1976, p. 11.

74. These views are derived from participation in negotiations and dialogue with negotiators in New York and Michigan, the two states which have pioneered community college collective bargaining. There is not much literature available on experience at the table. For bargaining tactics gleaned from the Michigan community college experience, see Ray A. Howe, "The Bloody Business of Bargaining," *College and*

University Business (March, 1970), pp. 63-67; see also Howe, "The Dramatic Action in Bargaining," *Faculty Bargaining in the Seventies*, ed. Terrence N. Tice (Ann Arbor: Institute of Continuing Legal Education, 1973), pp. 95-111.

On the New York experience, see George W. Angell, "Two Year College Experience," *Faculty Unions and Collective Bargaining*, eds. E.D. Duryea and Robert S. Fisk (San Francisco: Jossey-Bass, 1973), pp. 87-107. Angell makes the following insightful comment:

> Initially, presidents and trustees seldom expect faculty to challenge basic administrative prerogatives. They think that faculty will limit their serious demands primarily to salary and fringe benefits and use conventional deliberative campus approaches to the resolution of issues. Few of these expectations are fulfilled. Faculty are willing to use 'boiler plate tactics' from industry when opportune, to denigrate administrators and trustees whenever it is effective, and to insist that only they are capable of making intelligent decisions relative to academic matters. On the other hand, faculty expect most of their demands to appear reasonable to administrators and therefore acceptable to management with little debate. Such is seldom the case. As a result both parties feel offended and react negatively, slowing negotiations to the point of serious impasse. (p. 93)

Relevant Ph.D. dissertations on the negotiations process in these states include: Richard C. Creal, *A Study of Factors Which Influence the Course of Collective Negotiation Toward Resolution or Impasse in Selected Michigan Community Colleges* (University of Michigan, 1969); Richard J. Sullivan, *An Analysis of Collective Bargaining in Selected New York State Community Colleges, 1970-71* (State University of New York at Albany, 1972). There has not yet been a longitudinal study on behavioral change in this area.

75. For a similar, more fully developed view, see Thomas A. Kochan and Lee Dyer, "A Model of Organizational Change in the Context of Union-Management Relations," *The Journal of Applied Behavioral Science*, Vol. 12, No. 1, 1976, pp. 59-78.

76. For example, Joseph N. Hankin, "The Strategy and Tactics of Collective Bargaining," *Collective Negotiations in Higher Education*, ed. Michael Brick (New York: Columbia University, Community College Center, 1973), especially pp. 10-12.

77. Mike Yates and Bruce Williams, "What Radicals Can Do for the Teachers Unions," *Change* (Winter, 1974-75), p. 8.

78. Quoted, *Ibid*.

79. Ken Megill, "Loneliness and Solidarity," *Changing Education* (March, 1976), p. 11.

80. *Ibid*.

81. For example, see Fred E. Crossland, "Will the Academy Survive Unionization?" *Change* (February, 1976), pp. 38ff.

82. In 1976, legislation existed only at the state level. The Academic Collective Bargaining Information Service reported in Spring, 1976 that 24 states have bargaining laws covering community college faculty with most of these laws having been passed or amended in the last three years. Federal legislation to provide for public sector bargaining has been proposed.

83. See "Teachers on the Move for Unity and Political Action," *NEA Reporter* (August, 1974); also Albert Shanker, "A Full Employment Economy: Education's Life Line," *American Teacher* (September, 1975). Merger of these two unions has occurred on a local level.

The American Association of University Professors must be counted as the third large union. However, AAUP has been much more restrained in respect to consolidation, having firmly rejected merger proposals in the past although coalition has been accepted on a local level. Since AAUP does not have a strong constituency among community college faculties, the concern here is primarily with NEA and AFT.

A fourth large estate is formed by civil service employees unions, which also may have part of the action, particularly if federal legislation should pass in the future. The American Federation of State, County and Municipal Employees, like AFT, is affiliated with AFL-CIO.

84. Earl Latham, "The Group Basis of Politics: Notes for a Theory," *Political Behavior*, eds. Heinz Eulau *et. al.*, (New York: Free Press of Glencoe, 1956), p. 239.

85. Ladd and Lipset, *op. cit*.

86. In New York, it is clear that the simple fact of the legislation was a

strong factor in prompting most of the community college faculties to opt for bargaining agents. Partly due to this heavy flow, in 1973 New York was reported to be the "collective bargaining capital of the U.S.," containing about half of all the unionized faculty in the country. See J.W. Garbarino and M.W. Aussieker, "Creeping Unionism Re-Visited" in *Proceedings of the Twenty-Sixth Annual Winter Meeting*, Industrial Relations Research Association, December 28-29, 1973, p. 262.

87. This association numbered 16 faculty chapters in Spring 1976. There are 38 public community colleges in the state.

88. For an opposite evocation that illustrates briefly what the inde-pendent organizations are up against, see Robert Nielsen, "Counter-ing the 'No Agent' Vote," *American Teacher* (April, 1976), p. 17.

89. See Robert K. Carr and Daniel K. VanEyck, *Collective Bargain-ing Comes to the Campus* (Washington, D.C.: American Council on Education, 1973), p. 252.

90. Bargaining may occur, of course, without a recognized bargaining agent, but the main force is invested by legislation providing for elections.

91. For an explanation of why bargaining scope becomes broadened, see William F. McHugh, "Faculty Unionism and Tenure," *Collective Negotiations in Higher Education*, *op. cit.*, pp. 33-64.

92. See Robert D. Helsby, "Federal Legislation and Public Sector Bargaining," in *Proceedings of New York University Twenty-Eighth Annual Conference on Labor*, ed. Richard Adelman (New York: Matthew Bender, 1976), pp. 47-48.

93. Hankin, *op. cit.*, pp. 16-18

94. It is not meant to deny that the images of irrationality and exces-sive demands are a problem. For insight on how bargaining in some New York community colleges has affected trustees' perceptions of faculty and thereby the trustees' perspectives on their colleges' needs, see Rose Channing *et. al.*, "Collective Bargaining and Its Impact on Board-President Relationships," *Collective Negotiations in Higher Education, op. cit.*, pp.65-78.

95. Roger H. Garrison, *Junior College Faculty: Issues and Problems* (Washington, D.C.: American Association of Junior Colleges, 1967),

pp. 24ff.

96. Albert O. Hirschman, *Exit, Voice, and Loyalty* (Cambridge, Mass.: Harvard University Press, 1970), p. 81.

97. J. Vincent Baldridge and Frank R. Kemerer, *Unions on Campus* (San Francisco: Jossey-Bass, 1975), pp.207-208.

98. George W. Angell, Review of *Unions on Campus* in *Washington Report*, State University of New York Newsletter, ed. William Claire (May 1, 1976).

99. David W. Leslie, *Conflict and Collective Bargaining*, ERIC/ Higher Education Report No. 9 (Washington, D.C.: American Association of Higher Education, 1975), p. 15.

100. In addition to a plethora of articles, conference proceedings, and some thematic collections, four major comprehensive studies have been produced so far. Two of these were cited previously: Carr and VanEyck (1973), and Baldridge and Kemerer (1975). The others are: Everett C. Ladd, Jr. and Seymour M. Lipset, *Professors, Unions, and American Higher Education* (Washington, D.C.: American Enterprise Institute for Public Policy Research, 1973); Joseph W. Garbarino and M.W. Aussieker, *Faculty Bargaining: Change and Conflict* (New York: McGraw-Hill, 1975.) All of these studies are national in scope, cutting across all levels of higher education. There is a need for a similar empirical analysis devoted more exclusively to the distinctiveness of the community college segment.

The National Center for the Study of Collective Bargaining in Higher Education (Baruch College, City University of New York) compiles a complete bibliography on collective bargaining in higher education, which is distributed annually.

101. See Craig E. Polhemus, "Significant Decisions in Labor Cases," *Monthly Labor Review* (March, 1976), pp. 49ff.

102. Baldridge and Kemerer, *op. cit.*, p. 23.

103. Garbarino and Aussieker, "Creeping Unionism Re-Visited," *op. cit.*, p. 266.

104. Maurice Benewitz, "Bargaining in Higher Education," in *Proceedings of New York University Twenty-Seventh Annual Conference on Labor*, ed. David Raff (New York: Matthew Bender, 1975), p. 59.

105. Alan E. Bayer, "College Faculties: La Plus Ca Change," *Change* (March, 1974), pp. 49-50.

106. Baldridge and Kemerer, *op. cit.*, p. 105.

107. The effectiveness of faculty strikes needs more research, the results of which may contribute to settling this question. For a review of this issue, see "Exploring Alternatives to the Strike," Special Section, *Monthly Labor Review* (September, 1973), pp. 33-66.

CHAPTER VI

108. Abraham H. Maslow, Preface in Frank G. Goble, *The Third Force: The Psychology of Abraham Maslow* (New York: Pocket Books, 1970).

109. Ervin Laszlo, *The Systems View of the World* (New York: George Braziller, 1972), pp. vii-viii.

110. See Marjorie Grene, *Approaches to a Philosophical Biology* (New York: Basic Books, 1968), p. 226.

111. *Ibid.*

112. See Thomas S. Kuhn, *The Structure of Scientific Revolutions*, 2nd Ed. (Chicago: University of Chicago Press, 1970). Kuhn's work is subject to much criticism, some of which is dealt with in this second edition.

113. In 1976, the issue of research on recombinant DNA was brought forcefully to public attention at the University of Michigan and Harvard University in a fascinating and perhaps unprecedented way. At Harvard, for example, the Cambridge City Council, which had to rule on the building permit, heard sophisticated pro and con arguments. Following an intuitive or common sense approach, the mayor of Cambridge scheduled open debates and public demonstrations by scientists. The evidence of public participation in these matters, which has hardly even been sought in the past, was clearly visible.

114. It is interesting, nevertheless, that some of the most illustrious names in modern Western thought are associated with a serious interest in psychic phenomena, such as C.G. Jung, Wolfgang Pauli, William James.

More recently, the prominent marine biologist, Sir Alister Hardy, has made telepathy a major study. See Hardy, Robert Harvie and Arthur

Koestler, *The Challenge of Chance* (New York: Vintage Books, 1975).

It should also be noted that these comments pertain to science in Europe and America. Higher status given to parapsychology by science in the Soviet Union is reported by Sheila Ostrander and Lynn Schroeder, *Psychic Discoveries Behind the Iron Curtain* (Englewood Clifs, N.J.: Prentice-Hall, 1970).

115. Louisa E. Rhine, *ESP in Life and Lab* (New York: Collier Books, 1969), p. 262.

116. Arthur Koestler, *The Roots of Coincidence* (New York: Vintage Books, 1973), pp. 139-140.

117. Jonas Salk, *The Survival of the Wisest* (New York: Harper and Row, 1973), p. XI.

118. For an explanation of this point, see Kuhn, *op. cit.*, pp. 98ff.

119. *Ibid.*, pp. 118-119.

120. Exemplary of the call heard at both the state and national levels is a position paper adopted by the New York State Board of Regents in 1971 which states that "career education is an idea whose time has come, not in the sense that preparation for work should become the sole or even major focus of the educational process, but in the sense that student exploration of career interests, aptitudes, and abilities is a powerful means of effecting a much needed infusion of reality into the curriculum." The Board called for a comprehensive system which "continuously anticipates, perceives, and responds to employment problems." See *Occupational Education: Regents Position Paper #11* (Albany, N.Y.: State Education Department, May 1971), especially pp. 9-12.

121. See James O'Toole, "The Reserve Army of the Under-employed," I, II, in *Change*, Vol. 7, No. 4 (May, 1975) and Vol. 7, No. 5 (June, 1975); also Richard B. Freeman, *The Over-Educated American* (New York: Academic Press, 1976).

122. In 1970, Alvin Toffler quoted a U.S. Labor Department report on the occupation environment which requires "the average twenty-year-old man in the work force . . . to change jobs about six or seven times" during his working life. See Toffler, *Future Shock* (New York: Bantam Books, 1970), p. 109.

123. The role of higher education in fostering intellectual development — ideas — as an end in itself has unfortunately also been weakened by the loss of a vital liberal arts tradition, but even this concern is perhaps better approached by seeing any such uniquely aimed "liberal arts" programs under the umbrella of general education. The community college which feigns to give "liberal arts" education separate from general education is risking a false foundation for its curriculum development.

124. Daniel Bell, *The Reforming of General Education* (New York: Columbia University Press, 1966), p. 166.

125. Nicholas J. LoCascio, "Does Mortal Man Have the Right to Play God?" *The American Biology Teacher*, Vol. 35, No. 2 (February, 1973), p. 92.

126. An example of the ease of relating courses in the humanities is offered by a case of interaction between speech and English composition classes in which subject matter is outlined and discussed, after which papers are written by the English class. These papers are then read by the speech class as an oral interpretation exercise in joint session.

127. See Israel Scheffler, "Philosophies-of and the Curriculum," in *Educational Judgments: Papers in the Philosophy of Education*, ed. James F. Doyle (Boston: Routledge and Kegan Paul, 1973), pp. 209-218.

128. Salk, in his discussion of the model, clarifies that, whereas *metabiology* is intended to mean "beyond biology," *metaphysics* is not defined merely as "beyond physics." He indicates the broader significance of the term. See Salk, *op. cit.*, pp. 40ff.

129. See Billy Rojas and H. Wentworth Eldredge, "Status Report: Sample Syllabi and Directory of Futures Studies," in *Learning for Tomorrow: The Role of the Future in Education*, ed. Alvin Toffler (New York: Vintage Books, 1974), Appendix, pp. 345-399.

130. For example, see Michael Marien, *Alternative Futures for Learning: An Annotated Bibliography of Trends, Forecasts and Proposals* (Syracuse, N.Y.: Syracuse University Research Corporation, 1971).

131. For a summary of its origins and many-faceted development, see Paul Dickson, *Think Tanks* (New York: Ballantine Books, 1971).

CHAPTER VII

132. See Karl W. Deutsch, *The Nerves of Government: Models of Political Communication and Control* (New York: Free Press, 1966), p. 131.

133. There is no claim here to neo-Kantian expertise, a disclaimer made especially necessary when the effort to interpret is made through translations rather than original language. In Kant's moral writings, many questions are raised which have long been and are the subject of much debate. This conclusion seeks to gain from his writings, as translated by Kantian scholars, some assistance in a search for values within a general education construct.

134. Immanuel Kant, *Education*, trans. Annette Churton (Ann Arbor: University of Michigan, 1960), p. 11.

135. Immanuel Kant, "Religion within Limits of Reason," trans. Theodore M. Green and Hoyt Hudson, in *The Philosophy of Kant*, ed. Carl J. Friedrich (New York: Random House, 1949), p. 385.

136. *Ibid.*, p. 386.

137. Immanuel Kant, "Metaphysical Foundations of Morals," trans. Carl J. Friedrich, in *The Philosophy of Kant*, *op. cit.*, p. 159.

138. *Ibid.*, p. 173.

139. Kant, *Education*, p. 6.

140. Kant, "Metaphysical Foundations of Morals," *op.cit.*, pp. 182-184.

141. *Ibid.*, p. 148.

142. Kant, "Religion within Limits of Reason," *op. cit.*, pp.405-406.

143. Kant, "What is Enlightenment?", trans. Carl J. Friedrich, in *The Philosophy of Kant*, *op. cit.*, p. 132.

144. *Ibid.*, p. 133.

145. Kant, *Education*, p. 21.

146. See B. F. Skinner, *Beyond Freedom and Dignity* (New York: Vintage Books, 1971). The following excerpt serves as an interesting counterpoint in the discussion of Kant (or, contemporarily, of Maslow): "The struggle for freedom and dignity has formulated as a de-

fense of autonomous man rather than as a revision of the contingencies of reinforcement under which people live. A technology of behavior is available which would more successfully reduce the average consequences of behavior, proximate or deferred, and maximize the achievements of which the human organism is capable, but the defenders of freedom oppose its use. The opposition may raise certain questions concerning 'values.' Who is to decide what is good for man? How will a more effective technology be used? By whom and to what end? These are really questions about reinforcers. Some things have become 'good' during the evolutionary history of the species, and they may be used to induce people to behave for 'the good of others.' The challenge may be answered by intensifying the contingencies which generate behavior for the good of others or by pointing to previously neglected individual gains, such as those conceptualized as security, order, health, wealth, or wisdom." (pp. 119-120)

147. See Claude Lévi-Strauss, *The Elementary Structures of Kinship,* trans. James Harle Bell, John Richard von Sturmer and Rodney Needham, ed. (Boston: Beacon Press, 1969), pp. 478-497. It should be noted that the exchange system found at the origin of rules of marriage does not mean that the value in the exchange of women is simply that of goods. Rather, the exchange, in itself, has social value. "The law of exogamy is omnipresent, acting permanently and continually; moreover it applies to valuables — viz., women — valuables *par excellence* from both the biological and social points of view, without which life is impossible, or, at best, is reduced to the worst forms of abjection. It is no exaggeration, then, to say that exogamy is the archetype of all other manifestations based upon reciprocity, and that it provides the fundamental and immutable rule ensuring the existence of the group as a group." (p. 481)

148. Ervin Laszlo, "A Systems Philosophy of Human Values," *op cit,* pp. 250-251.

149. See Ervin Laszlo, *Introduction to Systems Philosophy* New York: Gordon and Breach, 1972), pp. 258 ff.

150. Ernest Becker, *The Birth and Death of Meaning: An Interdisciplinary Perspective on the Problem of Man,* 2nd Ed. (New York: Free Press, 1971), pp. 66, 79.

151. Ernest Becker, *The Structure of Evil* (New York: Free Press, 1968), p. 394.

152. Ernest Becker, *Escape from Evil* (New York: Free Press, 1975), p. 156.

153. *Ibid.*, p. 155.

154. Becker, *The Birth and Death of·Meaning*,p. 180.

155. Pierre Teilhard de Chardin, *The Phenomenon of Man,* trans. Bernard Wall (New York: Harper Torchbooks, 1959), pp. 284-285.

156. Becker, *The Birth and Death of Meaning*, p. 125.

157. Danilo Dolci's work in Sicily is perhaps a leading current example of Royce's view that man needs loyalty "because only in this way could he unite his life, his own history, and the history of his land and people." (Josiah Royce, quoted in Becker, *The Structure of Evil*, p. 265.)

158. Becker, *The Structure of Evil*, p. 268.

159. *Ibid.*, p. 269.

160. Ernest Becker, *The Denial of Death* (New York: Free Press, 1973), p. 284.

161. Becker, *The Structure of Evil*, p.270.

162. *Ibid.*

163. *The Letters of John Keats, op. cit.*, p. 316.

BIBLIOGRAPHY

Adelman, Richard, ed. *Proceedings of New York University Twenty-Eighth Annual Conference on Labor*. New York: Matthew Bender, 1976.

Angell, George W. Review of *Unions on Campus*, in *Washington Report*, State University of New York Newsletter, May 1, 1976.

Ardolini, Charles and Jeffrey Hohenstein. "Measuring Productivity in Federal Goverment," *Monthly Labor Review*, November, 1974.

Argyris, Chris. *Integrating the Individual and the Organization*. New York: John Wiley, 1964.

_____. *Intervention Theory and Method: A Behavioral Science View*. Reading, Mass.: Addison-Wesley, 1970.

Baldridge, J. Vincent and Frank R. Kemerer, *Unions on Campus*. San Francisco: Jossey-Bass, 1975.

Barbee, David E. *A Systems Approach to Community College Education*. New York: Auerbach, 1972.

Bayer, Alan E. "College Faculties: La Plus Ca Change," *Change*. Vol. 6, No. 2 (March, 1974).

Becker, Ernest. *The Structure of Evil*. New York: The Free Press, 1968.

_____. *The Birth and Death of Meaning: An Interdisciplinary Perspective on the Problem of Man,* 2nd Ed. New York: The Free Press, 1971.

_____. *The Denial of Death*. New York: The Free Press, 1973.

_____. *Escape from Evil*. New York: The Free Press, 1975.

Bell, Daniel. *The Reforming of General Education*. New York: Columbia University Press, 1966.

Bennis, Warren G. "The Concept of Organization Health." *General Systems Yearbook*, Vol. 7, 1962.

_____. *Changing Organizations*. New York: McGraw-Hill, 1966.

_____. *Organization Development: Its Nature, Origins, and Prospects*. Reading, Mass.: Addison-Wesley, 1969.

Bergquist, William H. and Steven R. Phillips. *A Handbook for Faculty Development*. Washington, D.C.: Council for the Advancement of Small Colleges, 1975.

Bertalanffy, Ludwig V. "General System Theory — A Critical Review," in Joseph A. Litterer, ed. *Organizations: Systems, Control and Adaptation,* Vol. II, 2nd Ed. New York: John Wiley & Sons, 1969.

Blake, Robert R. and Jane Syrgley Mouton. *The Managerial Grid*. Houston: Gulf Publishing Co., 1968.

Boulding, Kenneth. *Conflict and Defense: A General Theory*. New York: Harper, 1962.

_____. *The Meaning of the Twentieth Century: The Great Transition*. New York: Harper and Row, 1964.

Brady, Rodney H. "MBO Goes to Work in the Public Sector," *Harvard Business Review*, Vol. 51, No. 2 (March-April, 1973).

Brick, Michael, ed. *Collective Negotiations in Higher Education*. New York: Columbia University, 1973.

Burke, W. Warren. "Organization Development in Transition," *The Journal for Applied Behavioral Science*, Vol. 12, No. 1, 1976.

Caffrey, John, ed. *The Future Academic Community: Continuity and Change*. Washington, D.C.: American Council on Education, 1969.

Carr, Robert K. and Daniel K. Van Eyck. *Collective Bargaining Comes to the Campus*. Washington, D.C.: American Council on Education, 1973.

Churchman, C. West. *The Systems Approach*. New York: Dell, 1968.

Clark, Harold F. *Cost and Quality in Public Education*. Syracuse, N.Y.: Syracuse University Press, 1963.

Conant, James B. *Science and Common Sense*. New Haven: Yale University Press, 1951.

Copleston, Frederick. *Modern Philosophy*, Vol. 6, Part II (Kant) of *A History of Philosophy*. Garden City, N.Y.: Doubleday, 1960.

Coser, Lewis. *The Functions of Social Conflict*. New York: The Free Press, 1956.

Deegan, Arthur X. and Roger J. Fritz. *MBO Goes to College*. Boulder, Co.: University of Colorado, 1976.

Deutsch, Karl W. *The Nerves of Government: Models of Political Communication and Control*. New York: The Free Press, 1966.

Deutsch, Morton. *The Resolution of Conflict: Constructive and Destructive Process*. New Haven: Yale University Press, 1973.

Dewey, John. *Art as Experience*. New York: Capricorn Books, 1958. Original copyright, 1934.

Doyle, James F., ed. *Educational Judgments: Papers in the Philosophy of Education*. Boston: Routledge and Kegan Paul, 1973.

Drucker, Peter F. *The Practice of Management*. New York: Harper, 1954.

_____. "What Results Should You Expect? A User's Guide to MBO," *Public Administration Review*, Vol. 36, No. 1 (January/February, 1976).

Duryea, E. D. and Robert S. Fisk, eds. *Faculty Unions and Collective Bargaining*. San Francisco: Jossey-Bass, 1973.

Etzioni, Amitai W. *Modern Organizations*. Englewood Cliffs, N.J.: Prentice-Hall, 1964.

Feinberg, Walter. "Behavioral Theory and Educational Policy," *The Philosophical Forum*, Vol. VI, No 1 (Fall, 1974).

Ferkiss, Victor C. *Technological Man: Myth and Reality*. New York: George Braziller, 1969.

Forman, Maurice Buxton, ed. *The Letters of John Keats*. London: Oxford University, 1952.

Frazer, James G. "Human Sacrifices for the Crops," in Richard L. Cherry, Robert J. Conley and Bernard A. Hirsch, eds. *A Return to Vision*. Boston: Houghton Mifflin, 1971.

Freeman, Richard B. *The Over-Educated American*. New York: Academic Press, 1976.

Friedlander, Frank, "OD Reaches Adolescence: An Exploration of Its Underlying Values," *The Journal for Applied Behavioral Science*, Vol. 12, No. 1, 1976.

Friedrich, Carl J., ed. *The Philosophy of Kant: Immanuel Kant's Moral and Political Writings*. New York: Random House, 1949.

Fromm, Erich. *The Revolution of Hope: Towards a Humanized Technology*. New York: Harper & Row, 1968.

_____. *The Anatomy of Human Destructiveness*. Greenwich, Conn.: Fawcett Publications, 1973.

Garbarino, J. W. and M. W. Aussieker. "Creeping Unionism Revisited," in *Proceedings of the Twenty-Sixth Annual Winter Meet-*

ing, Industrial Relations Research Association, December 28-29, 1973.

Gardner, Howard. "France and the Modern Mind," *Psychology Today*, June, 1973.

Glueck, William F. *Organization Planning and Development*. New York: American Management Association, 1971.

Gouldner, Alvin W. "Organizational Analysis," in Robert K. Merton, Leonard Broom and Leonard S. Cottrell, Jr., eds. *Sociology Today: Problems and Prospects*. New York: Basic Books, 1959.

Grene, Marjorie. *Approaches to a Philosophical Biology*. New York: Basic Books, 1968.

Gross, Bertram M. *Oganizations and Their Managing*. New York: The Free Press, 1968.

Gulko, Warren W. *A Resource Requirements Prediction Model (RRPM-1): An Introduction to the Model,* TR-19. Boulder, Co.: National Center for Higher Education Management Systems, 1971.

Heinlein, Albert C., ed. *Decision Models in Academic Administration*. Kent, Ohio: Kent State University, 1973.

Henderson, Keith M. *Emerging Synthesis in American Public Administration*. Bombay: Asia Publishing House, 1966.

Hirschman, Albert O. *Exit, Voice, and Loyalty*. Cambridge, Mass.: Harvard University, 1970.

Homans, G. C. *The Human Group*. New York: Harcourt Brace, 1950.

Howe, Ray A. "The Bloody Business of Bargaining," *College and University Business*, March, 1970.

Hunter, John O. "Faculty Evaluation as a Liberal Persuasion," *Improving College and University Teaching*, Vol. XVII, No. 2 (Spring, 1969).

Kant, Immanuel. *Education*. Trans., Annette Churton. Ann Arbor: University of Michigan, 1960.

Kanter, Jerome. *Management-Oriented Management Information Systems*. Englewood Cliffs, N.J.: Prentice-Hall, 1972.

Koestler, Arthur. *The Roots of Coincidence*. New York: Vintage Books, 1973.

Kuhn, Thomas S. *The Structure of Scientific Revolutions*, 2nd Ed. Chicago: University of Chicago Press, 1970.

Ladd, Everett C., Jr. and Seymour M. Lipset. *Professors, Unions, and American Higher Education*. Washington, D.C.: American Enterprise Institute for Public Policy Research, 1973.

————. "The Growth of Faculty Unions," *Chronicle of Higher Education*, January 26, 1976.

Lahti, Robert E. *Innovative College Management*. San Francsco: Jossey-Bass, 1973.

Laszlo, Ervin and James B. Wilbur, eds. *Human Values and Natural Science*. New York: Gordon and Breach Science Publishers, 1970.

Laszlo, Ervin. *The Systems View of the World*. New York: George Braziller, 1972.

————. *Introduction to Systems Philosophy*. New York: Gordon and Breach Science Publishers, 1972.

————. "A Systems Philosophy of Human Values," *Behavioral Science*, Vol. 18,No. 4 (July, 1973).

Latham, Earl. "The Group Basis of Politics: Notes for a Theory," in Heinz Eulau, Samuel J. Eldersveld and Morris Janowitz, eds. *Political Behavior*. New York: Free Press of Glencoe, 1956.

Lau, James B. *Behavior in Organizations: An Experiential Approach*. Homewood, Ill.: Richard D. Irwin, 1975.

Leslie, David W. *Conflict and Collective Bargaining*, ERIC/Higher Education Research Report No. 9, Washington, D.C.: American Association for Higher Education, 1975.

Levinson, Harry. "Appraisal of What Performance," *Harvard Business Review*, Vol. 54, No. 4 (July-August, 1976).

Lévi-Strauss, Claude. *The Elementary Structures of Kinship*, Chapters I, II, XXIX. Trans., James Harle Bell, John Richard von Sturmer and Rodney Needham, ed. Boston: Beacon Press, 1969. Original copyright, 1949.

Likert, Rensis. *The Human Organization: Its Management and Value*. New York: McGraw-Hill, 1967.

Lippitt, Gordon L. *Visualizing Change: Model Building and the Change Process*. Fairfax, Va.: NTL Learning Resources, 1973.

Lock Land, George T. *Grow or Die: The Unifying Principle of Transformation*. New York: Random House, 1973.

Mark, Jerome A. "Meanings and Measures of Productivity," *Public Administration Review*, Vol. 32, No. 6 (November/December, 1972).

Maslow, Abraham H. *Religions, Values, and Peak-Experiences*. Columbus: Ohio State University Press, 1964.

_____. *Eupsychian Management: A Journal*. Homewood, Illinois: Richard D. Irwin and Dorsey Press, 1965.

_____. *Toward a Psychology of Being*, 2nd Ed. New York: D. Van Nostrand, 1968.

_____. *Motivation and Personality*, 2nd Ed. New York: Harper & Row, 1970.

_____. *The Farther Reaches of Human Nature*. New York: Viking Press, 1971

McGregor, Douglas. *The Human Side of Enterprise*. New York: McGraw-Hill, 1960.

Meeth, L. Richard. *Quality Education for Less Money: A Sourcebook for Improving Cost Effectiveness*. San Francisco: Jossey-Bass, 1974.

Mendelsohn, Everett and I. Bernard Cohen, eds. *The Social Context of Science: Readings for Social Sciences*. Cambridge, Mass.: 1966.

Merton, Robert K. "Priorities in Scientific Discovery," *The Sociology of Science: Theoretical and Empirical Investigations*, ed., Norman W. Storer. Chicago: University of Chicago Press, 1973.

Millett, John D. "Higher Education Management Versus Business Management," *Educational Record*, Vol. 56, No. 4 (Fall, 1975).

Morsch, William C. *Cost Analysis of Occupational Training Programs in Community Colleges and Vocational Training Centers*. Washington, D.C.: Bureau of Social Science Research, 1971.

Moynihan, Daniel P. "Goals, Systems and Hidden Policies," *The Futurist*, August, 1970.

Murphy, Jeffrie G. "Kant's Concept of a Right Action," in Lewis White Beck, ed. *Kant Studies Today*. La Salle, Ill.: Open Court, 1969.

Nagel, Ernest. "Mechanistic Explanation and Organismic Biology," in Baruch A. Brody, ed. *Readings in the Philosophy of Science*. Englewood Cliffs, N.J.: Prentice-Hall, 1970.

Nisbet, Robert. *The Social Philosophers: Community and Conflict in Western Thought*. New York: Thomas Y. Crowell, 1973.

O'Banion, Terry. *Teachers for Tomorrow*. Tucson: University of Arizona Press, 1972.

Odiorne, George S. *Management by Objectives*. New York: Pitman, 1965.

_____. *Management and the Activity Trap*. New York: Harper & Row, 1974.

Ortega, José y Gasset. *Mission of the University*. Trans., Howard Lee Nostrand. New York: W. W. Norton, 1944.

Ostrander, Sheila and Lynn Schroeder. *Psychic Discoveries Behind the Iron Curtain*. New York: Bantam Books, 1970.

O'Toole, James. "The Reserve Army of the Unemployed: I-The World of Work," *Change*, Vol. 7, No. 4 (May, 1975).

Pirsig, Robert M. *Zen and the Art of Motorcycle Maintenance*. New York: William Morrow, 1974.

Polhemus, Craig E. "Significant Decisions in Labor Cases," *Monthly Labor Review*, March, 1976

Potter, Van Rensselaer. *Bio-Ethics: Bridge to the Future*. Englewood Cliffs, N.J.: Prentice-Hall, 1971.

Raff, David, ed. *Proceedings of New York University Twenty-Seventh Annual Conference on Labor*. New York: Matthew Bender, 1975.

Rehfuss, John. *Public Administration as Political Process*. New York: Charles Scribner's Sons, 1973.

Rhine, Louisa E. *ESP in Life and Lab*. New York: Collier Books, 1969.

Richardson, Richard C., Clyde E. Blocker, and Louis W. Bender. *Governance for the Two-Year College*. Englewood Cliffs, N.J.: Prentice-Hall, 1972.

Rodin, Miriam and Burton Rodin. "Student Evaluation of Teachers," *Science*, Vol. 177, No. 4055 (September 29, 1972).

Rubin, Milton D., ed. *Systems in Society*. Washington, D.C.: Society for General Systems Research, 1973.

Salk, Jonas. *The Survival of the Wisest*. New York: Harper & Row, 1973.

Schein, Edgar H. *Organzational Psychology*. Englewood Cliffs, N.J.: Prentice-Hall, 1965.

————. *Process Consultation: Its Role in Organization Development*. Reading, Mass.: Addison-Wesley, 1969.

Seaborg, Glenn T. "Public Service and Human Contributions," *Oppenheimer*. New York: Charles Scribner's Sons, 1969.

Seiler, John A. *Systems Analysis in Organizational Behavior*. Homewood, Ill.: Richard D. Irwin and Dorsey Press, 1967.

Shane, Harold G. *The Educational Significance of the Future*. Report Prepared for Sidney P. Marland, Jr., U.S. Commissioner of Education. Washington, D.C.: World Future Society, October, 1972.

Skinner, B.F. *Beyond Freedom and Dignity*. New York: Vintage Books, 1971.

Teilhard de Chardin, Pierre. *The Phenomenon of Man*. Trans., Bernard Wall. New York: Harper Torchbooks, 1959.

Thomas, Lewis. *The Lives of a Cell: Notes of a Biology Watcher*. New York: Bantam Books, 1974.

Tice, Terrence N., ed. *Faculty Bargaining in the Seventies*. Ann Arbor: Institute of Continuing Legal Education, 1973.

Toffler, Alvin, ed. *Learning for Tomorrow: The Role of the Future in Education*. New York: Vintage Books, 1974.

Toffler, Alvin. *Future Shock*. New York: Bantam Books, 1970.

Watson, James D. *The Double Helix*. New York: Signet Books, 1968.

Whitehead, Alfred North. *The Aims of Education*. New York: Macmillan Co., 1929, 1957.

INDEX

Academic mission 7, 22-24, 28, 42, 44, 104, 114-115
Accountability
  defined 2-3
  legislated 3-4, 7, 11
Adaptation 1, 6, 68, 70, 128
Allegiance 72, 82-83, 86-87, 94
Angell, G. W. 84, 145, 148, 155
Arbitration 89-90, 92
Argyris, C. 46, 142, 143, 155
Attrition, tracking 34-35

Baldridge, J. V. and Kemmerer, F. R. 84, 89, 92, 148, 149, 155
Becker, E. 56, 129-132, 153-154, 155
Behavioral objectives 24, 139
Bell, D. 106, 112, 151, 155
Bennis, W. G. 5, 61, 97, 136, 143, 155
Bertalanffy, L. V. 96, 155
Blake, R. R. and Mouton, J. S. 48, 67, 141, 156
Boulding, K. 15, 65-66, 138, 143, 156
Bureaucracy 4-8, 11, 56
B-Values (Maslow) 58-60, 69, 71, 72

Career education 102-103, 150
Centralization
  effect of legislated accountability 7
  and unionism 79-82, 146
Collective bargaining
  as limitative model 75-78
  legislation 7, 80, 81-82, 146
  major issues 82, 84, 88-93
College environment 1, 3, 44, 53-54, 105
Conant, J. B. 101, 156
Commager, H. S. 95
Community
  and individual 55, 62-63, 71-72, 100
  college as model 5-6, 53-54, 56-57, 63
  education 56-57, 113, 119-120
  and unionism 80
  dignity and integrity 121-122

God-centered   131
Conflict resolution   15-16, 36, 58, 62-63, 65-68, 72, 87-88
Cost-simulation   36-38, 54
Curriculum development model   23

Deegan, A. X. and Fritz, R. J.   12-13, 20, 137, 138, 156
Delphi method   114, 139
Dewey, J.   49-51, 53, 54, 121, 127, 141, 157
Deutsch, K.   152, 156
Deutsch, M.   65, 143, 157
Drucker, P.   12, 136-137, 142, 157
D-Values (Maslow)   59-60, 65

Energy Problem   5, 111
Etzioni, A.   17, 138, 157
Evaluation
    faculty   42-48, 51-53, 54, 86, 91
    administrative staff   47-48
    program   39-42, 140
    group   44-47

Fromm, E.   62, 65, 142, 143, 157
Futures study   100, 103, 108, 111-113, 119, 151

Garbarino, J. W. and Aussieker, M. W.   90, 146-147, 148, 157-158
General education
    and basic skills   46-47, 118-119
    revitalization   101-103, 106-110, 113-117
    values of   71-72, 103, 107, 111-112, 127
General Scholarship   104-105, 117-120
General Systems Theory   96-97, 128-129
Glueck, W. R.   21, 138, 158
Goldstein, K.   96, 142-143
Grene, M.   97, 149, 158
Gross, B. M.   38, 140, 158
Growth
    and regression   63-65
    qualitative   67-68

Holistic thinking   96
Homans, G. C.   136, 143, 158

164